JAMES MADISON'S
MONTPELIER

HOME *of the* FATHER *of the* CONSTITUTION

Edited by Evelyn Bence

*The creation of this book was made possible
by a generous grant from
Mr. and Mrs. Charles H. Seilheimer, Jr.*

James Madison's
MONTPELIER

ACKNOWLEDGMENTS

The Montpelier Foundation would like to acknowledge the contributions of the following individuals in producing this book: Michael C. Quinn, Peggy Seiter Vaughn, Elizabeth Loring, Julia Stevens, Tom Chapman, John Jeanes, Gardiner Hallock, Maggie Wilson, Matthew Reeves, Adam Marshall, Allison Deeds, Susan Borchardt, Grant Quertermous, Cheryl Brush, Beth Taylor, Ann Miller, Mark Wenger, and Jeff Amstutz and Michael Miller at A2Z Design.

The Foundation also owes a great debt of gratitude to Evelyn Bence for taking information from a wide variety of experts and sources and forming it into a coherent and readable whole.

THE MONTPELIER FOUNDATION

James Madison's Montpelier survives as a 2,650-acre estate in Orange County, Virginia. Since the fall of 2000, it has been under the stewardship of The Montpelier Foundation, a private non-profit organization whose primary mission is to present the lasting legacy of James Madison as Father of the U.S. Constitution, Architect of the Bill of Rights, and president of the United States. To accomplish this, the Foundation is developing Montpelier as a place to learn about Madison's legacy and his vision of a constitutional government that is upheld by engaged citizens.

James Madison's Montpelier is a National Trust Historic Site.

NATIONAL TRUST **FOR HISTORIC PRESERVATION**®

ISBN Ø-9713261-2-6

PCN 2008931609

CONTENTS

"Who are the Best Keepers

of the People's Liberties?

The people themselves.

The sacred trust can be no

where so safe as in the hands most

interested in preserving it."

James Madison

1792

Welcome to
JAMES MADISON'S
MONTPELIER
HOME *of the* FATHER *of the* CONSTITUTION

J AMES MADISON'S HOME IS NOW ACCESSIBLE TO AMERICANS FOR THE FIRST time in a century and a half. The five-year restoration, completed in 2008, was a "forensic" process of recovery that successfully brought back every detail of the home that James and Dolley Madison created and loved. And their vision is impressive: over a span of three building campaigns, the Madisons created a home that is stunning for its architectural boldness, grandeur, unity, proportion, and design.

James Madison's lasting legacy is in the world of political theory, governmental structure, and individual rights. As the "Father" of the Constitution and "Architect" of the Bill of Rights, Madison was the genius of our nation's founding who gave us a system of government that—for the first time in history—achieved the ideals for which a revolution was fought. Madison's ideas truly transcend time and place.

Yet the restored Montpelier is the place to learn about James Madison, about his ideas, his life, and his personality, and about Dolley Madison. It is also a place to learn about the American Constitution and the principles of self-government and individual liberty that informed its creation and are the lifeblood of its continued success.

We have created this book to provide a history of Montpelier and those who resided here—and an account of all there is to see and do while you are here. This first edition also includes a section on the restoration, describing the passionate search for accuracy, the remarkable science, and the unparalleled craftsmanship that have made the restoration one of the finest and most exacting ever carried out.

I hope you will encounter the legacy of James and Dolley Madison on your visit. I hope you will glimpse the power of the Constitution, its effect on our lives, and its enduring greatness. And I hope you will be captivated by the beauty and inspiration of the place James and Dolley Madison called home.

*We the People of the United States, in Order to form
a more perfect Union, establish Justice, insure domestic
Tranquility, provide for the common defense, promote
the general Welfare, and secure the blessings of Liberty
to ourselves and our Posterity, do ordain and establish
this Constitution for the United States of America.*

PREAMBLE, U.S. CONSTITUTION

INTRODUCTION
MONTPELIER:
HOME OF THE FATHER
OF THE CONSTITUTION

The U.S. Constitution exists primarily because of the mind and career of James Madison. More than any of the other Founding Fathers, James Madison was the thinker whose innovative ideas laid the foundation for America's unprecedented form of government, leading him to be called the Father of the Constitution in his lifetime.

It was at Montpelier where Madison meticulously and exhaustively read, researched, and analyzed past democracies and why they had failed. It was here, gazing west to the Blue Ridge Mountains and America's future, where he devised an innovative and daring plan to balance power among three branches of government, among states large and small, between federal and state governments in order to unite thirteen distinct, parochial states into one union, lasting and strong. The consequences of his immense political and intellectual creativity and leadership still resonate today. Almost 220 years after the Constitutional Convention, the U.S. Constitution's radical principles continue to inform and influence the realities of American life and serve as a model for the world.

Montpelier was James Madison's beloved lifelong home. Here he was raised; here he brought home his young bride, Dolley; here he retired after his presidency. And at Montpelier he died, surrounded by the books and papers that meant so much to him in life.

Today Montpelier, restored to reflect Madison's full vision, is intended as a national monument to James Madison, the man who, by the force of his intellect, dedication, character, humility, and political skill, proposed our republic, and in so doing became ever after known as the Father of the Constitution. Montpelier is a place where American citizens can learn about the man, his home, and the Constitution that is his lasting legacy.

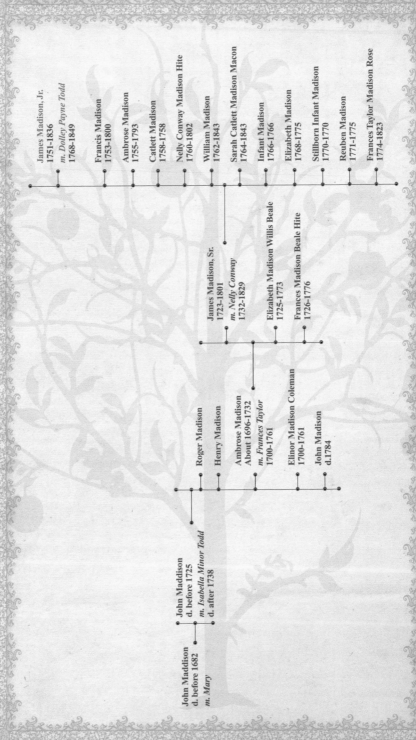

CHAPTER 1
A FAMILY'S LEGACY

BEFORE DELVING INTO THE HISTORY AND INTRIGUES

of the *place* known as Montpelier, we want to introduce the people—

the ancestors and family of President James Madison and the several

generations of enslaved workers—who lived on this plantation in the

beautiful Southwest Mountains of Virginia's Piedmont.

THE EARLY MADISONS

By the time James Madison—who would envision a new nation's federal republic—was born in 1751, his paternal family had resided and owned land in Virginia for nearly a century. The first record of the family name appears in 1653. John Maddison, a ship's carpenter, received six hundred acres of land in exchange for paying the Atlantic passage of twelve people. At his death, John owned a total of 1,900 acres in Virginia's Tidewater region.

His son, John, Jr., great-grandfather of the famed James, served as a justice of the peace in King and Queen County, indicating the family's growing social and economic position among Virginia's early landed gentry.

James' Grandparents: Ambrose and Frances Taylor Madison

In 1721, Ambrose Madison, the third son of John, Jr., married Frances Taylor, linking his future to another prominent colonial family, the Taylors. Five years earlier, Colonel James Taylor

had joined Governor Alexander Spotswood's westward expedition, crossing the Blue Ridge into the Great Valley of the Shenandoah. As one of these "Knights of the Golden Horseshoe" explorers, James Taylor was impressed with the rich forests and red earth of Virginia's Piedmont region. Taylor himself patented several large tracts of land in the Piedmont. An accomplished land surveyor, he was practiced in identifying rich farm land. Following his example, in 1723, his sons-in-law, Thomas Chew and Ambrose Madison, patented 4,675 rolling acres in what is now Orange County—land that included the future Montpelier.

Ambrose had three years to make improvements to receive final title to the acreage. To meet these legal requirements, Ambrose sent an overseer and a slave crew to clear land and erect a house and outbuildings. In 1726, an inspection and appraisal by neighbors showed that Ambrose Madison not only met the governor's requirements; he also ranked among the wealthiest men in the Virginia Piedmont.

In the spring of 1732, Ambrose and Frances, their son, James, and two younger daughters moved to their new plantation, which they named Mount Pleasant. Their household inventory included silver spoons, books, and a large stock of writing paper. That very summer, bad fortune struck. On July 31, knowing he was dying, Ambrose made out a will. He specified a life estate in Mount Pleasant for his wife, Frances, with the property passing to their son, James (Sr.), upon his reaching majority.

On August 27, 1732, Ambrose died. A single court document reveals that three enslaved African Americans were convicted of conspiracy to poison and murder Ambrose. Pompey, who had been on lease to Madison from a neighbor, was hanged; Turk, and a

Ambrose Madison's will.

woman named Dido, both owned by the Madisons, were sentenced to twenty-nine lashes and returned to Ambrose's widow, Frances.

Ambrose Madison's will and inventory at the time of his death serve as the two most important documents of the early history of Mount Pleasant, a family home that was vacated and abandoned soon after Montpelier was built. The archaeological record has also been an invaluable source of historical information.

After her husband's death, Frances managed the thriving and expanding tobacco plantation until her son, James (Sr.), assumed responsibility, apparently when he turned twenty-one in 1744. Frances never remarried, and for years continued to oversee the entire household and the raising and selling of crops. Dying in 1761, she never knew that her grandson James Madison would be instrumental in creating a new nation and lead it as fourth president, or that her brother's grandson, Zachary Taylor, would serve as the nation's twelfth president. She never knew that her western frontier plantation would someday become an east coast place of pilgrimage for disciples of liberty, students of history, and devotees of beauty.

James' Parents: James and Nelly Conway Madison

James Madison, Sr., a man of great talent and enterprise, ran a prosperous plantation even as he established other ventures—a distillery, a plantation store, a construction business, and an ironworks. He served as a vestryman of the local Anglican church, a justice of the county court, a sheriff, a road surveyor, and eventually as a colonel in the militia.

In September 1749, he married Nelly Conway, the daughter of Francis Conway, a merchant and farmer who lived south of Fredericksburg. Nelly settled into the Madison household but went back to her mother's home for the arrival of her first child, born March 16, 1751. Later that spring she and the new baby, named James, Jr., returned home to Mount Pleasant.

Portraits of Nelly Conway Madison and James Madison, Sr., painted by Charles Peale Polk in 1799.

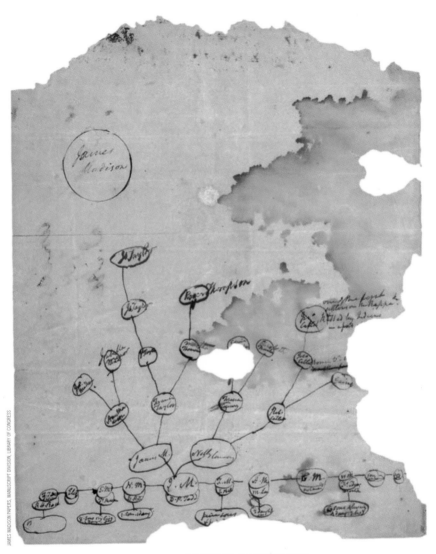

James Madison drew this inverted Madison family tree (above) extending back four generations. The bottom line represents the twelve children of James, Sr., and Nelly. James put himself in the middle, his sisters to the left and brothers (including two unnamed infants as "son") to the right. The paper is torn; a line extending off the page apparently represents brother Reuben, born in 1771.

JAMES MADISON
The Formative Years

James Madison, Jr., was the oldest of twelve children (seven surviving to adulthood). His grandmother Frances and his mother, Nelly, were no doubt his first teachers, supplemented by local clergymen and schoolmasters. As his father and grandmother enlarged the family library by ordering new volumes, young James laid the groundwork for his lifelong intellectual pursuit.

James' early years encompassed the Piedmont's hardships—a severe drought in 1755 and a smallpox epidemic in 1761, the year his grandmother Frances died at age sixty-one.

About this time, James, Sr., set a new course for his growing family by building a larger brick home on a hill about four hundred yards from the original Mount Pleasant farmhouse. James Madison recalled that as a boy he helped move small pieces of furniture from the old house to the new—which would later become known as Montpelier. James, Sr., and Nelly would live in the house from about 1764 until their deaths—James at age seventy-seven in 1801, and Nelly at age ninety-seven in 1829—more than a decade after her son had *retired* as president.

James Madison by Charles Willson Peale. Watercolor on ivory, 1783.

Eleven-year-old James was sent east to the Tidewater region to attend a boarding school run by a Scottish minister, Donald Robertson. For five years, he was immersed in a rigorous academic curriculum: learning Latin and Greek, reading the classics, studying mathematics, geography, French, and logic. James thrived in this environment and later credited Robertson: "All that I have been in life I owe largely to that man."

Returning to Montpelier, he studied privately with an Anglican rector for two years before forging a path different from many of his Virginian contemporaries. Instead of attending the College of William and Mary in Williamsburg, he decided to enroll in his tutor's alma mater, the "enlightened" College of New Jersey (now Princeton University). James' health may have

The old capitol building in Williamsburg, Virginia.

contributed to this decision; he later claimed he was constitutionally ill-suited for the steamy, low-lying Tidewater region.

In 1769 at age eighteen, James traveled with his enslaved manservant, Sawney, to Princeton where he continued his liberal arts education, delving into rhetoric, logic, and moral philosophy— laying the groundwork for his reasoned arguments in later years.

Completing Princeton's studies in just two years, Madison stayed on a third year for advanced study under its president, John Witherspoon.

As the oldest son, James likely helped his father manage the plantation he would eventually inherit. Like his father, he supported the colonial protests against excessive British taxation, but politics was not yet his passion.

Public Service Beckons

In 1774, Madison escorted a younger brother to Philadelphia and was in that city when word came that the British intended to blockade Boston's port in retaliation for the "Tea Party." The outrage that swept through Philadelphia spurred Madison the patriot; he returned to Montpelier eager to take a more active role in Virginia's pursuit of freedom and found his cause in the issue of religious liberty.

After the First Continental Congress of 1774, Madison worked in Orange County as a member of the provisional county government, called the Committee of Safety, and as a member of the militia. In 1776, he attained his first political office when he was elected as a delegate to the

MADISON'S INFLUENCE ON RELIGIOUS LIBERTY

Madison biographer Ralph Ketcham notes that "religious liberty stands out as the one subject upon which Madison took an extreme, absolute, undeviating position throughout his life."

Before the American Revolution, the colony of Virginia had an officially established religion—the Church of England or Anglican Church. The Madisons were members, attending services at the Brick Church, the Anglican church about six miles from Montpelier. Ambrose's library contained prayer books, and biblical commentaries from England. As for young James, the Scottish Presbyterian professors at the College of New Jersey and Quakers in neighboring Pennsylvania exposed him to different expressions of faith.

Back at Montpelier in 1774, James wrote an expressive letter to William Bradford, a college friend from Pennsylvania (and an eventual U.S. attorney general), condemning the arrest and jailing of "well meaning men" in a nearby county who had published "their religious Sentiments." These were probably Baptist ministers who had been preaching or praying illegally. Madison hoped for "Liberty of Conscience to revive among us."

As a delegate to the 1776 Virginia Convention, the junior Madison suggested profound changes to a proposed Virginia bill of rights, proclaiming the right to "the free exercise of religion" rather than "the fullest toleration in the exercise of religion." Over the next decade, he joined forces with Thomas Jefferson in enacting Virginia legislation that disestablished the Anglican Church from the state. Most notably, at Montpelier in 1785, he wrote *Memorial and Remonstrance against Religious Assessments*, a pamphlet that helped sway public opinion against a proposed "church tax." In this publication, he broadened his views to include liberty of conscience for those having no faith. Its success enabled Madison to introduce and get passed the Virginia statute for religious freedom that Jefferson had written ten years earlier.

Eventually the First Amendment of the U.S. Constitution—in the Bill of Rights, drafted by Madison— would forthrightly state: "Congress shall make no law respecting an establishment of religion, or prohibiting the free exercise thereof."

Virginia Convention that wrote the state's first constitution. He was subsequently appointed to several legislative committees and to the Council of State, which advised the governor. His political work in Williamsburg began his lifelong friendship with Thomas Jefferson.

Starting in 1780, Madison served for about four years as a Virginia delegate to the Continental Congress in Philadelphia. In Congress, he worked effectively—not as an orator (he had a soft voice), nor as an intimidating man of action (he was five-feet-four and somewhat retiring), but as a powerful intellectual force: drafting documents, working for public land rights and French support for America, arguing for responsible fiscal reform, serving on the Board of Admiralty, and negotiating relations among states.

The view of the Blue Ridge Mountains from the Old Library on the second floor of James Madison's home.

The American constitutional system is more the product of the mind and career of James Madison than of any other individual.

Father of the Constitution

Through the mid-1780s, Madison returned to the Virginia House of Delegates, dividing his time between Richmond, the new commonwealth capital, and his Orange County residence. At Montpelier, most likely in the second-floor Old Library with a view of the Blue Ridge Mountains, he embarked on a remarkable research project: studying every recorded attempt at self-government—rule by the people—and organized government rather than by a monarch. He pored over books shipped to him from Paris by Thomas Jefferson, the U.S. ambassador to France. Madison's research was driven by his growing awareness of the failings of the founding 1781 Articles of Confederation, under which the nation was loosely governed. As George Washington noted, "Thirteen sovereignties pulling against each other, and all tugging at the federal head, will soon bring ruin on the whole."

As Madison read, he analyzed: Why had all past democracies and federations eventually failed? What would work? Why? How could the interests of individuals, states, and the national authority be balanced? What was the real purpose of government?

He also worked with others to call for a "federal" convention that would be authorized to revise the Articles of Confederation. Finally, Madison persuaded George Washington to

TOP: *Signing of the Constitution* by Thomas Pritchard Rossiter, circa 1860-1870.
ABOVE: The Virginia Plan.

> *"Never wandering from his subject into vain declamation, but pursuing it closely, in language pure, classical, and copious, soothing always the feelings of his adversaries by civilities and softness of expression, [Madison] rose to the eminent station which he held in the great National Convention of 1787."*
>
> —*Thomas Jefferson*

The Constitution of the United States.

attend the Convention in Philadelphia, which gave it an importance lacking in the previous attempt at Annapolis, and ensured that every state would participate.

In May 1787, the Virginia delegation arrived in Philadelphia early and quickly rallied around Madison's proposal to frame a new, stronger national government, an "extended republic." His proposal was introduced as the Convention opened and became known as the Virginia Plan.

At the Convention, Madison spoke strongly for his positions, proposed compromises to bridge differences, and took copious notes. His intellect, preparation, political savvy, and behind-the-scenes persuasion led to many of his concepts being integrated into the U.S. Constitution, including representation in the House of Representatives according to population, a strong national executive, the need for checks and balances among three branches of government, and a federal system that assigned certain powers to the national government and reserved others for the states and the people.

MADISON'S PLAN GAVE US

> A House of Representatives elected by the people
> A strong national executive
> Checks and balances among three branches of government
> A federal system with specific powers to the national government, reserving others for the states and the people

MADISON ALSO:
> Drafted the Bill of Rights
> Authored *The Federalist* papers (with Alexander Hamilton and John Jay)

To persuade the people of the states to ratify the Constitution, Madison joined Alexander Hamilton and John Jay in New York to write a series of newspaper essays later known as *The Federalist* papers. Some of the Constitution's most formidable opponents, including George Mason and Patrick Henry, were from his own Virginia, so Madison returned home to take part in Virginia's ratifying convention. His views prevailed, and Virginia ratified in June 1788, the month the Constitution became the law of the land, with nine states having signed on.

In early 1789, Madison was elected as a member of the House of Representatives in the new Congress, and George Washington was elected the first president of the United States. For help with his first inaugural address, Washington turned to James Madison to draft his speech.

George Washington, lithograph from the original portrait painted by Rembrandt Peale.

LIBRARY OF CONGRESS, PRINTS AND PHOTOGRAPHS DIVISION

"The advice nearest to my heart and deepest in my convictions is that the Union of the States be cherished and perpetuated."

—*James Madison, 1834,* Advice to My Country

When Congress decided to reply, whom did they choose to draft their response? James Madison. And when Washington then replied to the House, he again turned to his friend, James Madison!

As a member of the first House of Representatives, Madison kept a promise he'd made to his fellow Virginians: he drafted and introduced amendments to the Constitution that would safeguard individual rights. Ten of these amendments, ratified in 1791, became the Bill of Rights, providing the mortar that helped cement the new relationships among the states, the people, and their new national government.

Ultimately Madison would be called Father of the Constitution and the Architect of the Bill of Rights for his leading role in the creation of these founding charters of the American nation.

Husband and Gentleman Farmer

In 1794, as a third-term Congressman—and forty-three-year-old bachelor—James Madison met the young, vivacious woman who would transform his life: Dolley Payne Todd. Dolley was a twenty-six-year-old widow, and mother of a two-year-old boy. Within months, James and Dolley were married. Madison continued his congressional duties in Philadelphia, where one fellow congressman noted, "Mr. Madison has been married … which event or some other, has … rendered him much more open and conversant."

Madison decided to retire from Congress after the conclusion of his fourth term in 1797. He settled his family—Dolley, stepson John Payne Todd, and Dolley's younger sister Anna Payne—into the Montpelier homestead, one of the largest plantations in Orange County. At home, he busied himself overseeing construction of an addition on the house for his family and helping his father in the management of the plantation's farms and businesses. Yet he

TOP: The Bill of Rights, passed by Congress on September 25, 1789. ABOVE: Pastel portraits of James and Dolley Madison drawn from life by James Sharples, Sr., in 1796-1797.

MADISON, THE MARINES, AND THE BARBARY PIRATES

"To the shores of Tripoli." The familiar phrase of the Marine Hymn refers to a U.S. Marine Corps engagement in Northern Africa during James Madison's term as secretary of state. For decades, pirates of the Barbary States had preyed upon merchant ships sailing the Mediterranean. The United States and European governments had paid "tributes"—extortion money—for protection. But in 1801, the Barbary pirates demanded even higher payments. The United States refused. The pirates declared war. Consulting with Madison, President Jefferson did not back down. For four years, the U.S. Navy skirmished with the pirates. Finally in 1805, the Marines took a major pirate base, successfully defeating them.

At an annual birthday ceremony,

placing a presidential wreath on Madison's grave, U.S. Marine Col. James M. Lowe noted that it was "James Madison's influence and recommendation" to confront the pirates on the shores of Tripoli. As president, Madison would again call on the Marines during the War of 1812, to fight against the British Navy. Madison, "a visionary and faithful friend to the Marine Corps," realized "the vital role we would play as 'soldiers of the sea' in defense of our nation."

remained a close observer of national politics and, with his friend Jefferson, grew more concerned about the direction that America's "great experiment" in democracy was taking under the administration of John Adams.

Secretary of State

In the presidential election of 1800, John Adams was defeated by the Republican candidate, Thomas Jefferson. When he took office in 1801, Jefferson appointed his trusted friend James Madison to the critical role of secretary of state. From the new capital of Washington, Madison negotiated international relationships

FROM TOP: Thomas Jefferson, by Gilbert Stuart, 1805. James Madison, by John Vanderlyn, 1816. James Monroe, by John Vanderlyn, 1816. BELOW: *View from Northeast of Fire-Damaged White House,* aquatint by George Munger, 1814.

in a tense age. England, Napoleon's France, and Spain all vied for power in Europe, on the open seas, and in the New World. In protest of the resulting shipping and trade abuses, the Jefferson administration pushed for an embargo of foreign goods, particularly those from Britain. As a team, three Founding Fathers—President Jefferson, Secretary of State Madison, and emissary James Monroe—nearly doubled the size of the United States in 1803, strategically purchasing from France the Louisiana Territory—the land west of the Mississippi to the Rocky Mountains.

Mr. Madison, Mr. President

At the conclusion of Jefferson's two terms, James Madison won the 1808 presidential election and took the oath of office the following March. Madison's first term was troubled by tensions between England and France that led British ships to forcibly stop U.S. trading ships and seize American seamen. Furthermore, frontiersmen blamed the British for stirring up American Indian resistance to western settlement, and some expansionists had sights on Canada.

Finally giving up on a policy of economic coercion, the United States declared war on Britain on June 18, 1812. After severe American losses on the Canadian front, the British marched on Washington. Madison rode east from the White House to review the American troops and,

as fighting broke out, became one of the few U.S. presidents to command on the field of battle. His efforts failed and, on August 24, 1814, the British burned the U.S. Capitol and the White House. Leaving Washington, the British then launched a naval bombardment of Fort McHenry in Baltimore. The assault failed, but the battle inspired Francis Scott Key to pen the words to *The Star-Spangled Banner*, which would become the nation's anthem.

The Taking of the City of Washington in America. An 1814 wood engraving of the capital city under attack by British forces.

Four months later, December 24, 1814, the warring parties settled on terms of peace. In what some have called the second war of independence (and what opponents dubbed "Mr. Madison's War"), the War of 1812 solidified the United States' place within the international community.

Known for his personal integrity and fair-handedness, Madison scrupulously observed individual and political rights even in the midst of war. As the Capitol and White House were rebuilt, the last years of Madison's second term saw economic growth, westward expansion, and ushered in a nationalistic "era of good feeling."

Building a Legacy

After his second term, sixty-six-year-old Madison stepped aside, and fellow Virginian James Monroe won the presidential election in 1816. James and Dolley happily returned home to Montpelier, where he would spend his remaining years.

During his retirement, James actively managed his five-thousand-acre plantation. In the mornings, he surveyed the farm fields and work yards of the plantation, riding his horse named Liberty. At this time, Montpelier was supported by cash crops (tobacco and wheat), gardens, and livestock

Therm. sunrise	Wind sunrise	Weather sunrise	Therm. A OCPM	Wind A OC.PM	Weather A(
41	NE	cloudy ground thinly covered with snow	48	NW	fair. snow gone
42	SW	fair	58	S.	fair
52	E.	cloudy	53	NE	light rain
58	SW	clouds breaking away after very rainy night	59	SW	fair & windy after 2 s... from S.W.
52	S.W	fair	59	from W&NW	flying clouds, extremely
50	E	fair	58½	N	fair
48	NE	cloudy 8 OC. rain, 2 OC. rain & Hail	46	S.W	snowing, ground nearly
38	SW	clear. Blue ridge covered with snow	44	from W to NW	flying Clouds Wind bl...
40	S.W.	fair	44½	W	flying clouds, stron...
44	N	fair	53	N	fair
48	E.	fair	52	E.	cloudy
47	E	cloudy	47½	NE	very light rain sun...
48	E	fair	50	W	flying clouds
46	SW	fair	50	W	broken clouds
48	SW	fair	56	NW	fair

James Madison's meteorological journal kept at Montpelier. This page, in Madison's own handwriting, dates from the end of March to the beginning of April 1785.

(beef, sheep, and hogs) large enough to sustain the family, the daily guests, and approximately one hundred enslaved workers living on the plantation. Madison experimented with the latest agricultural techniques, including rotating crops, soil amendments, testing new plant varieties, and inter-planting fruit trees among grain fields. He tracked rainfall and daily temperatures and compared his findings with those of his close friend Thomas Jefferson. He also served as president of the Albemarle Agricultural Society in 1818.

Madison's public service did not end when he returned to Virginia. He joined with Jefferson in founding the University of Virginia and succeeded him as the rector (president) of the University after Jefferson's death in 1826. In 1829, he served as a delegate to the state convention in Richmond that drafted a new Virginia Constitution. And in the 1830s, he accepted the honorary presidency of the American Colonization Society, which worked to return emancipated slaves to their African homeland after purchasing their freedom from slave owners.

In his retirement, Madison dedicated himself to another great research project: creating an archive of the Constitutional Convention. At the Convention, he had taken thorough notes of each day's deliberations; now he returned to those notes, using them as a basis for a detailed account of the Convention. He also incorporated notes and speeches from other delegates. Madison believed that a record of "the opinions & reasoning" that went into the Constitution's creation would be an aid to America's understanding of it and an aid

View of the University of Virginia, Charlottesville and Monticello by E. Sachse & Co., 1856.

"In social intercourse, no one could be more delightful than Mr. Madison . . . In my latest visits to him, when confined to the bed or sofa in the next room, he would invite me to take his place at the table; and call out, that if I did not pass the wine more freely, he would 'cashier' me!"

—Robley Dunglison

to "the cause of Liberty throughout the world," helping people in other countries or in the future when faced with the need to create their own governments. His record of the Convention ultimately approached a thousand pages in length.

Madison scrupulously honored the pledge he made at the Convention to keep its proceedings secret until the death of all delegates. This meant his papers could not be published until after his death, but he realized that publication might bring much-needed financial help to Dolley. Crop failures, a severe economic downturn, the expense of extending hospitality to hundreds of guests, and the profligacy of John Payne Todd, the grown and dissolute son of Dolley, had drained his finances.

Engraving of James Madison by Thomas B. Welch from a drawing by James B. Longacre made at Montpelier in July 1833. It is the last life portrait of Madison known to have survived.

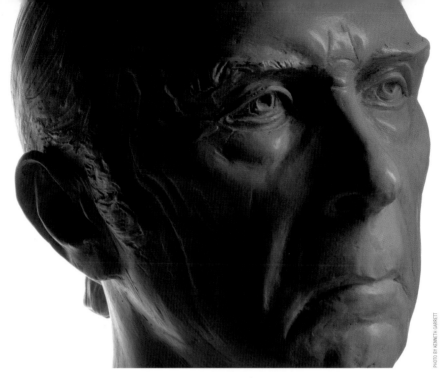

Madison was seventy-four years old when John Browere covered his face with plaster to make a life mask from which a bust was sculpted. Robert Shure created this 1998 plaster reproduction of the 1825 original.

In his final years, Madison, who had often suffered bouts of ill health, grew increasingly frail, often bedridden as a result of arthritis. Yet he remained mentally astute, and visitors found him willing and eager to discuss the issues of the day.

At the age of eighty-five, James Madison died on June 28, 1836, at Montpelier, propped up in a daybed in what is now called Mr. Madison's Room, surrounded by the books and papers that constituted so much of his life's work. With him were his niece Nelly Willis and his enslaved personal attendant, Paul Jennings. In his memoir, Jennings reported that Madison had trouble swallowing his breakfast that morning. When Nelly asked him what was wrong, James replied, "Nothing more than a change of mind, my dear." Jennings then recounted that Madison's "head instantly dropped, and he ceased breathing as quietly as the snuff of a candle goes out." The next day Madison was buried in the family cemetery, a quarter mile south of his treasured house.

DOLLEY MADISON
Madison's Bride

As a bachelor, James Madison underook the work that won him acclaim as the Father of the Constitution, but it is hard to imagine his continued political success without the spark and skill of his beloved wife, Dolley. Hailing from old Virginia families, Dolley's parents, John and Mary Coles Payne, lived in North Carolina when Dolley was born on May 20, 1768. She spent her childhood in Hanover County, Virginia. An ardent Quaker, her father freed his slaves in 1783 and sold his Virginia farmlands. He then moved his large family to Philadelphia, the nation's capital. He proved ineffective as a laundry-starch merchant and to make ends meet, the family took in boarders, including Congressman Aaron Burr, a college classmate of Madison's.

Portrait of Dolley Madison by Alan Dordick, after Gilbert Stuart.

In 1790, Dolley married an up-and-coming Quaker lawyer, John Todd. They had two sons, John Payne (called Payne) and William. But tragedy struck the young family when yellow fever swept through Philadelphia in 1793. Dolley's husband and her infant son William died on the same day, leaving twenty-five-year-old Dolley a widowed single mother with a two-year-old son.

In May 1794, Congressman James Madison asked his colleague Aaron Burr to introduce him to the charming widow Todd. Dolley excitedly wrote a note to a childhood friend, "The great little Madison has asked . . . to see me this evening." James was love-struck. Dolley, younger by seventeen years, seemed to consider more practical concerns. Anticipating marriage, she wrote a friend: "In this union I have everything that is soothing and greatful in prospect—& my little Payne will have a generous & tender protector."

James and Dolley married in September 1794 at Harewood, the Virginia (present-day West Virginia) home of Dolley's sister Lucy, who

was married to George Washington's nephew, George Steptoe Washington. James and Dolley honeymooned near Winchester, Virginia, at Belle Grove, the plantation of James' sister Nelly Hite. With James' responsibilities as a member of Congress, the Madisons resided in Philadelphia until 1797, when the family, along with Dolley's younger sister Anna, moved to the rural Montpelier homestead—out of the limelight, but not for long.

Political Hostess

In 1801, when the Madisons moved to Washington—ninety miles north of Montpelier—the nation's new capital was hardly more than a few government buildings and a plan. Boarding houses accommodated politicians whose families had not moved to town. The Madisons lived briefly in the president's house with Jefferson, a widower. Even after the Madisons moved to their own home, several blocks away on F Street, Dolley often returned to the president's house to serve as Jefferson's hostess. Dolley became the center of the new Washington social scene by spending afternoons "calling" on other residents and, with her sister Anna, hosting dinners at the Madison home.

TOP: Dolley Madison, 1872 engraving by Alonzo Chappell after the portrait by Gilbert Stuart. ABOVE: *Lewis and Clark with Sacagawea at the Great Falls of the Missouri*, painted by Olaf Seltzer in 1804.

COURTESY OF GILCREASE MUSEUM TULSA, OKLAHOMA

In 1803, when funds ran short to outfit Lewis and Clark's expedition through the Louisiana Territory, Dolley informally took up the cause; she successfully rallied enough local donations to outfit the "Corps of Discovery" with essential supplies and gear. Upon returning three years later, the explorers thanked the Washington women, presenting them with souvenirs of their western journey.

A WAR HEROINE
IN THE WHITE HOUSE

The Madisons usually spent the hot summer months, when the government was in recess, back home at Montpelier. But not in 1814, when Washington itself was in peril of being attacked by the British. After initial optimism of the capital's safety, many residents evacuated Washington in mid-August as British troops threatened. As a precaution, the White House staff, including slave Paul Jennings, started packing up and shipping out valuables. Then, just after midnight on August 24, the president received a message from Secretary of State James Monroe: "The enemy are in full march on Washington." Mr. Madison rode off to inspect the defensive preparations. After her husband's departure, Dolley and her staff kept packing "cabinet papers" even while hopefully preparing dinner for guests, as planned. Bravely ignoring all warnings, she remained in the house.

Ultimately Dolley fled, but not until an urgent rider arrived with a message from Madison: "Clear out, clear out!" She still refused to depart until a full-length portrait of George

Washington was safely spirited out of harm's way. "I have ordered the frame to be broken, and the canvass taken out," she wrote her sister. That night British troops dined on the Madisons' dinner before torching the home. The soldiers reportedly looted a portrait of Dolley—to show and brag about in London—but her patriotic respect for history spared the prized portrait of the "Father of the Country" a similar fate.

In an era that was both patriarchal and extremely partisan, Dolley Madison was also known for her diplomatic skill of quietly brokering compromise by inviting political adversaries to dinner. In her home, northerners

The "Lansdowne portrait" of George Washington, painted by Gilbert Stuart in 1796 and saved from the British by Dolley Madison in 1814.

PHOTO BY KENNETH GARRETT

William John Coffee sculpted this small portrait bust of Dolley Madison during an 1818 visit to Montpelier.

and southerners, Federalists and Republicans, diplomats and frontiersmen ate and conversed, breaking down assumed stereotypes and promoting civility.

When Madison was elected president in 1808, an opponent tellingly noted, "I was beaten by Mr. and Mrs. Madison. I might have had a better chance had I faced Mr. Madison alone."

"The Presidentess"

The first inaugural-night ball in Washington, D.C., was held upon James Madison's taking office. Madison—Mr. President—looked pale and soon tired; Dolley took center stage, wearing a white turban accessorized with bird-of-paradise feathers. Acknowledging her regal, yet not royal, status, the *National Intelligencer* dubbed her "the Presidentess."

Dolley set out to bring a lively social life to her husband's administration. She decorated the still-unfinished presidential home on Pennsylvania Avenue with the help of architect Benjamin Henry Latrobe, introducing a novel style based on the ancient décor being discovered in excavations at Pompeii. The style evoked the ancient Greek and Roman sources

"Habit and hope are the crutches which support us through the vicissitudes of life."

—*Advice the matronly Dolley Madison wrote in then-popular autograph books*

of democracy and captured the country's imagination. The *Baltimore Whig* solidified a new term of endearment: " 'White house' may be considered the 'people's name' " for the president's home. To reinforce the notion of it being the people's house, she hosted weekly open houses. Visitors from every part of the nation, locals, and members of Congress dropped in, and Mrs. Madison's "Wednesday Nights," soon became an essential part of the political scene of the nation's new capital.

History remembers Dolley Madison for her composure and courage as the British invaded Washington in 1814 and burned the White House and U.S. Congress. Her inspiring presence also helped galvanize support for the rebuilding and revitalization of Washington as the capital city. She was active in many organizations. She was the founding "directress" of the Washington Female Orphan Asylum, created to help the poorest in the city. From their temporary homes after the invasion, the Madisons viewed the reconstruction and enlargement of the White House, a building they were never to re-occupy.

Dolley Madison shaped the culture of the nation's capital by setting both political and social precedents for the new federal city in Washington, establishing a dignified, but uniquely democratic tone. Her warmth, grace, tact, and political and social flair coupled with her husband's intellect, position, and political skills made the pair a force in Washington and in our nation's history.

Montpelier Hostess

After Monroe's inauguration in March 1817, the Madisons left Washington with their household goods to return to Montpelier. At age forty-eight, Dolley may not have been ready to "retire," and in some ways she did not. She continued to entertain neighbors, the large extended family, and other guests at occasions small and large. On July 4, 1816, James and Dolley entertained

POLLY THE TERRIBLE

Visitors to Montpelier were impressed by the household's most colorful character: a macaw named Polly who spoke—and sometimes screamed and swore—in French. The bird was also a menace, lunging at and pecking guests and terrorizing children. One visitor, Judith Walker Rives, was grateful that Mr. Madison intervened to protect her, but was horrified to see Polly bite his finger "to the bone—a catastrophe which gave me real sorrow, though he took it in perfect good humor, as only [being] pretty Polly's way."

Eventually the tables were turned on Polly; as an old bird, she herself was caught and clutched as prey for a hawk.

THE FIELD MUSEUM, CNYO797. GPLEP_003_010

Blue and Yellow Macaw, engraving by Edward Lear.

AN ERRANT SON: JOHN PAYNE TODD

Reflecting on the Madisons' final retirement at Montpelier, Dolley's cousin Edward Coles noted a "serpent in the Garden of Eden"—her errant and only son, John Payne Todd (1792–1852).

When they married, James took Dolley's two-year-old son as his own and by all accounts was a dutiful, even indulgent, father. When the Madisons lived in Washington, Payne attended a Catholic boarding school in Baltimore. During Madison's second term as president, twenty-one-year-old Payne served as secretary to an official U.S. delegation to Europe. During these travels, through Russia, France, Belgium, England, and the Netherlands, Payne acquired many pieces of art that found a home at Montpelier. But his parents also received distressing reports of his irresponsible escapades. Madison biographer Ralph Ketcham notes, "From this time on Todd was increasingly a financial drain and psychic strain on both his mother and stepfather"—drinking, gambling, and wandering in and out of the family circle.

Madison paid out over $40,000 to Payne's creditors, at least half of this without Dolley's knowledge. Even so, Payne twice landed in debtors' prison—breaking his mother's heart.

Payne's debts and irresponsibility contributed to the dismantling of the formerly prosperous Montpelier. When widowed Dolley moved to Washington, Payne sold valuable possessions. He muddled the publication of James' papers and contested the provision in Dolley's will that left a bequest to her companion niece.

History remembers John Payne Todd as a man highly beloved by his doting mother—and hardly anyone else.

John Payne Todd, engraving after a watercolor on ivory, circa 1820.

ninety "at one table, fixed on the lawn, under a large arbor." The setting suited her: "I am less worried here with a hundred visitors than with twenty-five in Washington." In time, even uninvited travelers stopped by to meet the "Sage of Montpelier," prompting Madison to keep a spyglass on the front Portico to identify the occupants of incoming carriages.

For the next nineteen years, James and Dolley stayed close to home, traveling no farther than Richmond, and there only once, in 1829, just months after the death of James' mother Nelly, so James could participate in drafting a new constitution for Virginia. Dolley missed the urban bustle of Washington, but she would not leave her beloved James, who preferred the Virginia

"Madison and I often run races here [on the Portico], when the weather does not allow us to walk." —Dolley Madison, as reported by a Montpelier visitor

countryside. One insider reported, "They look like Adam and Eve in Paradise." For years, Dolley worked alongside James, serving as his secretary and editor, even as she managed the slaves who worked to feed and clothe the household. As James' health deteriorated, Dolley's teenaged niece Annie Payne came to live at Montpelier and stayed with Dolley for the rest of her life.

Mrs. Madison Returns to Washington

James died in June 1836. In November 1837, Dolley returned to Washington, leaving Montpelier in the hands of her son, Payne. For several years, she spent summers at Montpelier, even as she mortgaged the property and sold off parcels to keep the plantation afloat. But her financial situation did not improve, and in 1844 she regretfully sold the family property, including some of the slaves. A few of the slaves remained with her and served as household staff in Washington.

In Washington, Dolley—now wearing "vintage" dresses and turbans—was soon

Daguerreotype of Dolley Madison made by Mathew Brady, 1848.

society's grand lady, welcomed into homes and events, the honored and effervescent guest. A living symbol of the generation of the Founders, she was granted an honorary seat in the House of Representatives. Her death in July 1849 occasioned the largest state funeral Washington had experienced.

MONTPELIER'S ENSLAVED COMMUNITY
Slave Life at Montpelier

James Madison was one of twelve children and the third generation of Madisons to make the Montpelier plantation home. Yet the size of his family does not compare to Montpelier's largest community: enslaved African

> *"The magnitude of this evil [slavery] among us is so deeply felt, and so universally acknowledged; that no merit could be greater than that of devising a satisfactory remedy for it."*
>
> —*James Madison to Frances Wright, September 1825*

Americans. During the Madison family's ownership (1723–1844), many generations of African Americans were born into slavery on the plantation. Grandfather Ambrose's estate inventory (1732) listed 29 slaves. In 1801, his son's estate included 108; under James, the number remained around 100.

Slaves worked from "can see" to "can't see," meaning from dawn to dusk, and in all weather. Like most Virginia slave owners, James afforded slaves time off on Sundays and other holidays. He told one Sunday guest that he could not expect "the servants to wait upon him, as they made it a holiday." One account mentions the slaves gathering on a Sunday for religious services: women wearing bright calicoes; umbrellas opening at the first drops of rain.

The "field slaves" of Montpelier did the hard manual work of planting, caring for,

COURTESY OF THE MONTPELIER FOUNDATION/LINDA BOUDREAUX MONTGOMERY

Interpretive painting of a slave funeral at Montpelier in the 1820s.

Interpretive painting of the South Yard, which housed Montpelier's domestic slaves.

and harvesting crops ranging from tobacco and grain to hemp and vegetables. They lived in crude cabins near the fields where they labored. Overseers (enslaved black or hired white men) received instructions from the master for the workforce in the overseer's assigned fields or "quarter."

Slaves with special skills—blacksmiths, carpenters, masons, grain and wood millers, teamsters, and weavers—worked alone or in small groups. When not needed at home, craftsmen were sometimes leased out to neighbors.

Other slaves served in domestic roles as house "servants," such as cooks, gardeners,

"We have seen the mere distinction of colour made in the most enlightened period of time, a ground of the most oppressive dominion ever exercised by man over man."

—*James Madison, at the Constitutional Convention, June 1787*

butlers, maids, and launderers. They lived with their own families in a complex very near the Madison's house—the South Yard—that featured small duplexes with wood floors and glazed windows—better housing than the field slaves. Rooms in the mansion cellars, outfitted with fireplaces, probably allowed enslaved domestic servants to be "on-call" for the Madison household and its guests.

Most slaves at Montpelier spent their entire lives there, along with the Madison family—but there were exceptions. When young James went off to college, a "personal servant" his same age named Sawney accompanied him. In his prime, Sawney, who, unlike many slaves, knew how to read, was overseer of a field tagged "Sawney's tract." He was trusted to leave the plantation to sell produce and buy supplies in Fredericksburg. In one letter, James instructed him to plant particular fields with potatoes rather than tobacco. In his old age, Sawney was a caregiver for the elderly Nelly, "Mother Madison."

The Madisons supplied basic housing and provisions for the slaves. In a letter to his father (November 1790), James gave instructions that an overseer, Mordecai Collins, should

"chuse out one of the Milch Cows for his own use, and let the rest be milked for the Negroes. To keep the Negros supplied with meal to be kept in a barrel apart for themselves: the barrel now there holding 13 pecks to be filled 3 time every two weeks. To receive from Sawney's 400 lb. of Pork for himself; one half of the remained to be for the Negroes at B. [Black] Meadow, as was the case last year."

To supplement these basic rations, slave families had small vegetable gardens near their cabins. Many also kept chickens. In the Madisons' retirement, Sawney often sold to

Letter from James Madison to his father giving instructions for overseer Mordecai Collins, November 1790.

LIBRARY OF CONGRESS, MANUSCRIPT DIVISION

Dolley eggs, chickens, and vegetables from his yard. Typically, enslaved men could fish and hunt small game for their families. Household items supplied by the master were supplemented from local markets and by barter-exchange.

Madison's View of Slavery

On moral grounds, James Madison was repelled by the institution of slavery. As early as 1785, Madison wrote that he wanted "to depend as little as possible on the labor of slaves." To that end, he rather unsuccessfully dabbled in land speculation and would later move away from planting high-maintenance tobacco. In 1785, he also fought against a bill that would have outlawed the manumission of any slaves in Virginia. On the national level, at the 1787 Constitutional Convention, Madison found the issue of slavery so contentious that he and others set it aside, realizing that it would derail the effort to unify the states into a single nation. To Madison, the creation and preservation of the union was preeminent.

Madison's philosophical rhetoric was strong. But, in reality, his grand plantation and hospitable Montpelier home was viable only because of its enslaved workforce. He could not imagine an alternative, and the best he could manage on a personal level was a paternalistic care for "his people." Madison's enslaved manservant, Paul Jennings, noted: "I never saw him in passion, and never knew him to strike a slave . . . neither would he allow an overseer to do it." If Madison heard of a slave causing trouble, he would "send for

WILLIAM GARDNER'S JOURNEY TO FREEDOM

A telling letter, from James to his father (September 1783), illuminates his struggle with the issue of slavery. James referred to William (Billey) Gardner, a personal slave who had been with him for three years in Philadelphia. Preparing to return to Montpelier, James wrote: "I have judged it most prudent not to force Billey back to Va. even if it could be done; and have accordingly taken measures for his final separation from me. I am persuaded his mind is too thoroughly tainted to be a fit companion for fellow slaves in Virginia." Pennsylvania laws allowed for the selling of slaves, but restricted servitude to seven years, followed by freedom. "I do not expect to get near the worth of him; but cannot think of punishing him by transportation [further south] merely for coveting that liberty for which we have paid the price of so much blood, and have proclaimed so often to be the right, & worthy the pursuit, of every human being."

James indeed sold Gardner, to a Pennsylvania Quaker. After achieving freedom, he became a merchant's agent. From Philadelphia he conducted business for the Madisons, but on a voyage to New Orleans Gardner suffered an untimely death by drowning. Madison wrote to his father back at Montpelier, "Please let old Anthony and Betty know their son is no more."

REMEMBERING PAUL JENNINGS

Born at Montpelier in the 1790s, Paul Jennings served in the Madison household, accompanying them to Washington during Madison's presidency. He became Madison's manservant in 1820 and attended him until the day he died.

When Dolley subsequently moved to Washington, she took Paul with her. Her will, written in 1841, provided: "I give to my mulatto man Paul his freedom." But her financial distress overrode her intention.

In 1846, Dolley sold Paul, a widower with children, to a Washington insurance agent; six months later he was sold again, this time to Dolley's former Lafayette Square neighbor, Senator Daniel Webster. Webster gave Paul his freedom papers, and arranged for him to work off his purchase price in 1847.

Paul became an important member of the free black community of Washington. In 1848, he surreptitiously helped to plot the unsuccessful escape attempt of seventy-seven slaves on the schooner *Pearl*. In 1849, he married

The E. & P. Perry Photograph Co.

COURTESY SYLVIA JENNINGS ALEXANDER

Desdemona Brooks, a free mulatto woman from Alexandria, Virginia. With Senator Webster's recommendation, Paul was employed by the Pension Office of the U.S. Department of the Interior. In 1863, a coworker, John Brooks Russell, contributed Jennings' reminiscences to a history journal. Two years later, they were published as a small book titled *A Colored Man's Reminiscences of James Madison*. In the memoir, Jennings described Madison as "one of the best men that ever lived," whose slaves "generally served him faithfully." On a more sobering note, he told of delivering food and gifts from Daniel Webster to the aged, impoverished Dolley and giving her money from his own pocket.

Paul owned a house in Washington, on L Street near 18th NW, where he lived with his son John and near his daughter, Frances. Son Franklin farmed in nearby Dumfries, Virginia. Both sons served the Union cause in the Civil War. According to Franklin, Paul died at home in May 1873, a gentle close to a long and eventful life.

them and admonish them privately." Madison instructed one overseer to treat his charges with "humanity and kindness," without forgetting "their necessary subordination."

Although Madison contemplated freeing his slaves, he never did so. He believed that, given past history, free blacks and whites could not live together in peace and that slaves should not be freed unless "they are permanently removed beyond the region occupied by, or allotted to a white population." To this end, he was a founding member, financial supporter, and honorary president of the American Colonization Society.

Ultimately, in his eighties and facing mounting financial problems, Madison sold sixteen slaves—with their permission—to a relative. Though he had reportedly indicated to an antislavery activist that his will would provide freedom for his slaves, that document left the slaves to his wife, Dolley, and stated only that they should not be sold without their consent and Dolley's. Ultimately Dolley also succumbed to financial pressure, selling a number of Montpelier's slaves with or without their permission.

C H A P T E R   2
A HOMESTEAD'S HISTORY

DETAILS OF MONTPELIER'S HISTORY ARE STILL BEING

discovered—beneath its green turf, in aging documents, in digital

analysis . . . But before delving into the mysteries revealed in

restoration and archaeological investigations, we address a basic

question about the "great little" Madison's lifelong home: How did

Montpelier develop into the grand estate we see today?

LINDA BOUDREAUX MONTGOMERY

TOP: **Artist's rendering of the Mount Pleasant homestead around 1732.**
ABOVE: **Montpelier archaeologists survey Mount Pleasant excavation site.**

MOUNT PLEASANT: PREDECESSOR TO MONTPELIER

In 1732, James Madison's grandfather, Ambrose, moved his family from Virginia's Tidewater to their new home, Mount Pleasant, built by his enslaved workers on land that would become Montpelier. By the twentieth century, all trace of the original Mount Pleasant buildings had disappeared. In 2001, an archaeological team discovered a building foundation in a field near the Madison Family Cemetery. Careful excavations over the next three years revealed the scope of the first plantation complex: a small two-room farmhouse for the family, a free-standing kitchen, storage buildings, slave quarters, barns, and work areas—home to three generations of Madisons over a thirty-year period.

The archaeological evidence suggests that the farmhouse burned around 1770, probably intentionally as a means of demolishing it, since all the valuable hardware had been removed before the fire. The kitchen may

have survived into the next century, as a map drawn in 1848 shows an overseer's house in the same general vicinity. The nearby cemetery dates to Ambrose's death in 1732 and today is the only remaining vestige of the first Madison home.

TOP: Conjectural elevation of the Mount Pleasant Madison house based on archaeological evidence. ABOVE: Household objects found by archaeologists at the Mount Pleasant site. From top: button, door lock part, pins and thimble, and flatware. ABOVE LEFT: Archaeologists reveal the stone-lined cellar of the Mount Pleasant home.

THE NEW HOUSE

James Madison, Sr., built the core of the Montpelier house around 1763–1765, creating the largest brick dwelling in Orange County. A planter, businessman, and county official, James, Sr., likely designed his house and supervised the crew of enslaved workers that erected it. Plantation records suggest that at least two slaves, George and Peter, were skilled carpenters.

The house consisted of a raised basement and nine rooms: four on the main floor and five upstairs, with hall passages on the first and second levels. On the first floor, the two front rooms were public rooms—a parlor and dining room. The two rear rooms and those upstairs were private or "family" rooms. All these rooms served multiple purposes, and, as is true today, their uses would have evolved with the needs of the household and changes in styles.

MONTPELIER: A MEANINGFUL NAME?

Although Mount Pleasant and Montpelier seem similar, no documentation links the two names. The name Montpelier appears no earlier than 1781, and even then in a sidelong reference in a letter written by Edmund Pendleton, who commented on "the Salubrious Air of [Mr. Madison, Sr.'s] fine Seat, not to be exceeded by any Montpelier in the Universe." By 1799, the name Montpelier was firmly established and being used by James, Sr., in a fire insurance policy.

James himself used the French spelling—Montpellier—suggesting a derivation from the town in southern France that was known for its ancient university and as a healthful resort. Contemporary use associates the name with a wholesome environment, which is reflected in an explanation provided by Margaret Bayard Smith, a close friend of the Madisons, that "The extreme salubrity of the situation induced the proprietor [James Madison] to call it Montpelier."

James, Sr., had his workers build brick walls to divide the grounds of the new home into three distinct areas: a service complex, including the kitchen, slave quarters, and garden, to the south; pleasure grounds in the central section; and to the north a blacksmith shop for the commercial

Computer model of the original (1763-1765) house.

James Madison, Sr., built the core of the Montpelier house around 1763–1765, creating the largest brick dwelling in Orange County.

manufacture and repair of farming equipment, horseshoes, saddle parts, hinges and locks, and guns and knives. The thriving blacksmith complex provided James, Sr., with a significant portion of his income. All the ironworkers were slaves, with an African American named Moses serving as the foreman-overseer.

MADISON'S DUPLEX

Thirty-five years after the home was constructed, James Madison, Jr., came home with Dolley, and began constructing a thirty-foot extension on the north end. This provided four additional rooms: a parlor (or bedroom) and dining room downstairs and two upstairs bedrooms. The addition had its own main entry and stair. A 1799 insurance policy gives the enlarged dwelling's dimensions as thirty-three by eighty-six feet and mentions its wood-shingle roof. As in the earlier house, the addition did not include a kitchen; instead, a new detached wood-framed kitchen was built to

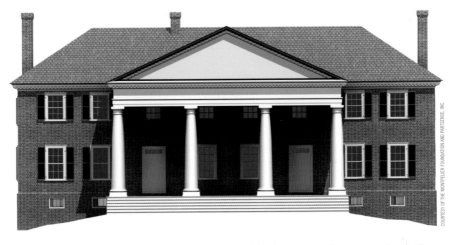

Computer model of the house after the 1797-1800 additions.

the north of the house, supplementing the earlier brick kitchen to the south.

A new two-story Tuscan portico enhanced and united the front of the house, looking west to the Blue Ridge. Apparently designed by Madison, the Portico seems to be the earliest two-story classically proportioned monumental portico on a house in Virginia. Two front doors, one leading into the original house and the other serving James' new addition, were "framed" by the portico columns.

This addition, in effect, made the brick building a duplex—two separate housing units with no interior doors between them on the

CABINET CONSULTATIONS

About the time Madison was enlarging Montpelier, his Albemarle County friends Thomas Jefferson and James Monroe were embarking on construction projects of their own: Jefferson renovating Monticello and Monroe building Highland (now Ash Lawn–Highland). Throughout the process, the three future presidents exchanged advice and workmen. In October 1798, Jefferson asked Madison to delay sending Mr. Richardson, the plasterer and mason, to Monticello for at least

and roofer), who would finish his job at Montpelier in time to work for Monroe.

Long after the initial Montpelier remodeling was otherwise completed, Madison and Jefferson were still corresponding about the finish of the portico columns. "Common [interior] plaister would not do," Jefferson noted. He advised that the columns should be "brick covered with stucco." But the columns remained "unfinished" until after 1807—about the time a new renovation plan for Montpelier was drawn up by master builder James Dinsmore under Madison's direction. Dinsmore had worked extensively for Thomas Jefferson.

a week, because he was not ready for him to begin. To Monroe, Madison recommended Reuben Chewning (probably a carpenter

ABOVE LEFT: Monticello, home of Thomas Jefferson. ABOVE RIGHT: Ash Lawn-Highland, home of James Monroe.

first floor. To get from one side to the other, the family had to go outside or upstairs. The senior Madisons lived in the original house on the south side of the building. James, Dolley, Payne, and Dolley's sister, Anna, occupied the new north section.

ABOVE: Computer model of the house after the 1809-1812 additions. BELOW: *Montpelier, Va. Seat of the Late James Madison*, engraving, 1836, showing the post-renovation appearance of the house and immediate grounds. J.F.E. Prud'homme after John Gadsby Chapman.

PRESIDENT MADISON'S HOUSE AND GARDEN

During his first term as president (1809–1813), James embarked on a third major Montpelier building campaign. After hiring three master craftsmen who had worked for Jefferson, he began renovations and additions that would remake the house into a dwelling fit for a president.

First, he merged the duplex, making it one house again, by creating a new central doorway, although the two existing front doors remained in place as flanking entrances. On the interior, he united the two homes by installing two arched doorways on the first floor. And he created a grand central Drawing Room by combining two of his father's rooms. He also refined the exterior of Montpelier by replacing and enlarging all but one of the windows.

More dramatically, James added one-story wings on both ends of the home, providing a suite for his mother on the south and a large room he intended for use as a library on the north. A deck or "terrace" was built on top of each wing, expanding the second floor living spaces. Cellar kitchens were created under both wings, one for James and Dolley on the north, and the other for Nelly on the south—introducing cooking facilities into the house for the first time.

Finally, a back (east) Colonnade was built, its roof also serving as a second-floor terrace overlooking the rear lawn.

About 1810, James' slaves excavated a deep pit in the North Yard to serve as an ice house. To cover the ice pit, workers built what is now known as Mr. Madison's Temple above it. Dolley's niece Mary Cutts noted that the Temple was "intended, but never used" as James' study. Another dramatic landscaping project involved leveling a knoll located between the rear Colonnade and the formal garden and using the soil to fill a gully behind the North Wing, to create a large, level rear lawn suitable for entertaining. An equally massive undertaking was terracing the formal garden—nearly four acres in size—to create planting beds arranged in a horseshoe shape.

James transformed Montpelier's landscape

BELOW: Massive cedar-of-Lebanon outside the formal garden at Montpelier. Tradition holds that this tree was a gift to the Madisons from the Marquis de Lafayette during his 1824 visit to Montpelier.

DOLLEY'S "BEAZEE BONNET"

Madison paid his French gardener Monsieur Bizet the then-enormous annual salary of seven hundred dollars. In a memoir published after Dolley's death, her niece Mary Cutts described the Bizets as being "great favorites" of the slaves, "some of whom they taught to speak French." Mary continued, "Madame [Bizet/Beazee] contrived a hat to shade Mrs. Madison's eyes; it was 'hideous,' but she liked it and when she took her morning rambles always called for her Beazee bonnet."

with picturesque naturalistic features that emphasized the beauty of the Virginia Piedmont, including broad lawns with large trees and outbuildings screened by plantings. He redesigned the front approach to the house, creating a new road that brought visitors through a wood, nearly a mile away, to a dramatic view of his expanded home. The front lawn was enclosed by an elegant picket fence that paralleled an older farm road. He created a semicircular, stone-paved carriage siding immediately in front of the house. A double row of white pines lined a path from the house to the new Temple. Madison corresponded with American and European horticulturalists and botanists and introduced some exotic plants, such as the English oak on the south lawn. Tradition holds that the large cedar-of-Lebanon near the entrance to the Annie duPont Formal Garden was given to James, after his retirement, by the people of France.

South of the house, a row of trees and shrubs shielded from view the South Yard—living quarters and work spaces of the household slaves. Beyond that, the new horseshoe-shaped terraced garden (now the Annie duPont Formal Garden) was filled with vegetables, fruit trees, flowers, and ornamental shrubs. Dolley's niece Mary Cutts remembered harvests of the "choicest" pears; she noted that James himself "liked to gather" the figs and grapes. "It was a paradise of roses and other flowers, to say nothing of the strawberries, and vegetables; every rare plant and fruit was sent to him by his admiring friends, who knew his taste, and they were carefully studied and reared by the gardener and his black aids."

MONTPELIER AFTER MADISON: THE NINETEENTH CENTURY

James Madison died in 1836, and eight years later Dolley sold Montpelier. Over the course of the nineteenth century, the property changed hands repeatedly.

The first owner, Richmond merchant Henry Wood Moncure, purchased not only the land and the house, but also some of the slaves and household furnishings.

Four years later (October 1848), Moncure sold Montpelier—again including some of the Madison furniture—to Benjamin Thornton of Gomersall, Leeds, England. Two Thornton daughters were born here, and their descendants have loaned to Montpelier many items believed to have belonged to the Madisons.

The Thorntons made a number of exterior changes to the house; most strikingly they covered the exterior bricks with a gray stucco that resembled granite. They also removed the front steps of the Portico and extended the columns to the ground. Over the wings, the flat terraces with their Chinese rail were also removed, as were the wood shingles on the center two-story section, and a new roof of standing-seam tin was installed. The effect was to transform Montpelier's classical design to one more in keeping with the latest Greek Revival style. During this transformation, the grounds in front of the mansion were also modified, removing the old carriage road and its picket

"No one I think can appreciate my feeling of grief and dismay at the necessity of transferring to another a beloved home."

—*Dolley Madison to Montpelier buyer Henry Moncure*

fence and bringing the curved entrance drive up to the Portico.

In January 1854, Montpelier was purchased by William H. Macfarland, a prominent Richmond banker who had delivered a noted eulogy after Madison's death. In an editorial, the *Fredericksburg News* commented, "it is to be hoped that a suitable monument may now be erected over the remains of Virginia's eminent statesman" now that the "estate has fallen into the hands of a Virginian."

Macfarland held the property only one year and sold it, without placing a marker at

An 1863 sketch of Montpelier by a Confederate soldier.

Madison's grave, to Colonel Alfred V. Scott, who moved his family from Alabama for a short period of two years.

In August 1857, the Scotts sold Montpelier to Thomas Carson, an Irish American banker in Baltimore. Soon after his purchase, the stone monument marking the gravesite of James Madison was installed, and Dolley Madison's remains were removed from Congressional Cemetery in Washington and re-interred next

to him; her grave was also marked with a monument. During the Civil War, Montpelier became the home of Thomas Carson's eccentric bachelor brother, Frank. Confederate troops camped on the property for eight months during the winter of 1863–1864, and many Confederate

ABOVE: Photograph (ca. 1885) of the front of the house showing the stucco and portico changes of the 1850s. BELOW: Photograph showing the rear of the house (ca. 1885). The dormers were added and the rear doors to the wings were closed sometime after the mid-19th century.

soldiers provided descriptions—and, in one case, a sketch—of the famous home. Fifteen years later, in 1878, Montpelier was visited by President Rutherford B. Hayes, who especially noted the extreme size and age of many trees surrounding the house.

When Frank Carson died in 1881, the property—showing evidence of neglect—was purchased by Louis F. Detrick, of Baltimore, and William L. Bradley, of Boston. The men were partners in a guano-fertilizer business, and they used Montpelier as a summer home for their families. Detrick and Bradley held the estate for nineteen years and redecorated extensively. An article in *Architectural Record* (1896–1897) noted that Montpelier's interior "has been remodelled out of all semblance to its original self."

Documentation indicates that most of the Madison-era outbuildings near the house had been cleared by 1900. As for the garden—its boundaries were greatly reduced, and the original beds and plantings were lost.

Computer drawing of the house (in color) and with later additions made by the duPont family early in the twentieth century.

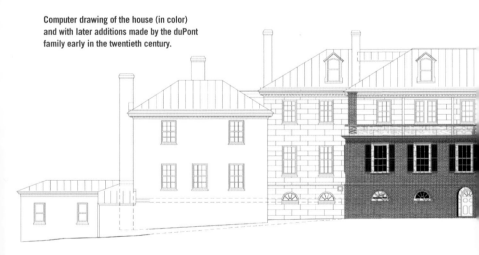

MONTPELIER OWNERS

> **The Madison Family**
> (1723–1844), 121 years
>> **Ambrose Madison**
>> (1723–1732), 9 years
>> **Frances Madison**
>> (1732–1761), 29 years
>> **James Madison, Sr.**
>> (1761–1801), 40 years
>> **James Madison, Jr.**
>> (1801–1836), 35 years
>> **Dolley Madison**
>> (1836–1844), 8 years
>
> **Henry W. Moncure**
> (1844–1848), 4 years
> **Benjamin Thornton**
> (1848–1854), 6 years
> **William H. Macfarland**
> (1854–1855), 1 year
> **Alfred V. Scott**
> (1855–1857), 2 years

> **Thomas J. Carson and Frank Carson**
> (1857–1881), 24 years
> **Louis F. Detrick and**
> **William L. Bradley**
> (1881–1900), 19 years
> **Charles King Lennig**
> (1900), 2 or 3 months
> **The duPont Family**
> (1901–1983), 82 years
>> **William duPont**
>> (1901–1928), 27 years
>> **Marion duPont Scott**
>> (1928–1983), 55 years
>
> **National Trust for Historic Preservation**
> (1984–Present)
> **The Montpelier Foundation**
> (Steward, 2000–Present)

THE DUPONT MANSION

Montpelier changed hands again in November 1900, when Charles King Lennig—William duPont's secretary and agent—purchased the property, which he formally transferred to William duPont in January 1901. Lennig oversaw renovations and new construction, and a year later the duPont family of four—William, his wife, Annie, and their children, William, Jr., and Marion—moved to Montpelier. Though the duPonts maintained other homes, they raised their children at Montpelier.

BELOW: Annie duPont with her dog in the back yard of the house. BOTTOM: Aerial view of the house during the duPont era.

The duPonts more than doubled the size of the Montpelier house, adding floors above the one-story wings and building additions behind the home. Mrs. (Annie) duPont furnished and decorated Montpelier after the family arrived in 1902, using chandeliers, mirrors, sofas, and tables she had selected from exclusive antique

shops while previously living in England. A selection of duPont furnishings is now displayed in the Visitor Center's William duPont Gallery.

Retaining the naturalistic, park-like landscape of the grounds, the duPonts added many exotic tree species, such as blue Atlas cedar and Nordmann fir. Today more than fifty different species of evergreens and deciduous trees create a remarkable arboretum on the mansion's grounds. The duPonts planted ornamental shrub beds, including rows of boxwood along the road in front of the house.

Their daughter, Marion, age eight when the family arrived in 1902, took ownership after her father's death in 1928 and made Montpelier her lifelong home. Married to and divorced from actor Randolph Scott, she went by the name Marion duPont Scott. A lifelong lover of horses, Marion transformed the property into a world-class thoroughbred racing stable, adding a number of barns, a training track, and a steeplechase course. Her steeplechase course crosses the expansive fields in front of the home and is the only American track to retain

TOP: William duPont, Jr., (Willie) and his sister, Marion. ABOVE: William duPont, Sr., at Montpelier.

ABOVE: Marion was the first woman to ride astride at a national horse show.

live brush jumps. Several of her prize-winning horses, including the famous Battleship, are buried near Mr. Madison's Temple, and their graves are marked with tombstones.

Inside the home, Marion renovated one room in the sleek Art Deco style in the 1930s and filled the room with photographs of her winning horses. She left the remainder of the home as her parents had built and furnished it.

In writing her will, Marion concluded that "it is appropriate" that the mansion should be restored "in such a manner as to conform as nearly as possible with the architectural pattern which existed when . . . owned and occupied by President Madison." After her death in 1983, her heirs transferred ownership to the National Trust for Historic Preservation in 1984, as she desired.

The National Trust opened Montpelier to the public in 1987. In 2000, the Trust transferred stewardship of Montpelier to The Montpelier Foundation through a long-term lease and other agreements, which paved the way for the restoration of the historic home as it was created by James and Dolley Madison.

COURTESY OF THE MONTPELIER ARCHIVES

PHOTOGRAPH BY JOHN STRADER

TOP: Photograph of the front of the house, ca. 2002, showing the enlargements made by William duPont. ABOVE LEFT: Marion duPont Scott in the original Art Deco Room. ABOVE: The annual Montpelier Hunt Races remain a cherished tradition.

CHAPTER 3
A HOME'S RESTORATION

AFTER ASSUMING STEWARDSHIP OF MONTPELIER,

The Montpelier Foundation determined that the question of

whether Montpelier could be restored should be resolved. Although

many elements of the Madison-era home were apparent, the full

construction history of the house was uncertain, as was the feasibility

of accurately and fully recovering the house as created and loved by

James and Dolley Madison.

CAN WE FORM A MORE PERFECT MANSION?

With the help of a generous grant from the estate of Paul Mellon, in 2001 The Montpelier Foundation embarked on a comprehensive architectural study of the Montpelier home. A research team went to work, opening some three hundred "study units" into the house—cutting holes in walls, lifting floorboards, and chiseling through stucco and plaster. Their findings were thoroughly documented, and samples of paints, wallpapers, wood, and nails carefully cataloged. Researchers also combed through old records, some previously undiscovered, such as an 1808 architectural drawing, visitors' descriptions, and nineteenth-century photographs. Especially important was the itemized invoice from the builder of the 1810 expansion. The investigation lasted eighteen months, intensively examining every aspect of the home. The Montpelier Foundation reviewed the findings with the assistance of a

Restoration Advisory Committee members discuss restoration. Left to right: Calder Loth, Mark Wenger, Willie Graham, John Jeanes, and Michael Quinn (seated).

RESTORATION ADVISORY COMMITTEE MEMBERS

> **Bill Beiswanger**, Monticello
> **Barbara Campagna**, Graham Gund Architect, NTHP (2006-2008)
> **William Dupont**, Graham Gund Architect, NTHP (2000-2006)
> **Willie Graham**, Colonial Williamsburg Foundation (2004)
> **John Larson**, Old Salem

> **Calder Loth**, Virginia Department of Historic Resources
> **Travis McDonald**, Poplar Forest
> **Dennis Pogue**, Mount Vernon
> **Orlando Ridout IV**, Maryland Historical Trust
> **Jim Vaughan**, National Trust for Historic Preservation

Restoration Advisory Committee composed of volunteer experts and concluded that the Madison home had survived largely intact and that it was possible to accurately restore the mansion to its nineteenth-century form.

After reviewing the study findings, The Montpelier Foundation concluded that restoring the home was the right thing to do: restoring Montpelier would enable the life and ideas of James Madison to be preserved and presented to the public in a unique way in the very space where he lived. The restoration would return the

Visitors touring restoration.

TOP: Steve Chronister carefully removes for storage the center portion of the original duPont gilded ceiling in the Morning Room.
ABOVE: Mark Wenger examines a study unit.

home to the one the Madisons created during James' presidency, when it reflected both his entire career and his full architectural vision for his home. The Restoration Advisory Committee concurred with this decision, as did preservation agencies at the state and federal levels. The National Trust for Historic Preservation, the Virginia Department of Historic Resources, the National Park Service, and the federal Advisory Council on Historic Preservation were all consulted, and all endorsed restoring the home. The Montpelier Foundation also consulted with the members of the family of William duPont and received their support and encouragement.

The estate of Paul Mellon again stepped in to make the dream a reality, this time pledging a grant of $20 million—$18 million of which would be used for restoration. In October 2003, the Foundation officially announced that the Montpelier mansion would be restored to the home of the Madisons.

EXTERIOR RESTORATION
Documenting and Deconstructing

Work began almost immediately with the preliminary task of thoroughly documenting the appearance of the existing duPont mansion. Every existing interior room was recorded with archival photography and video; paint colors, trim details, flooring, and other elements were noted and samples preserved. Lighting fixtures, doors, door hardware, and two stairways were removed and placed in storage. This "duPont Collection" is a permanent part of the collections of The Montpelier Foundation, ensuring that a full record of the evolution of Montpelier is preserved for future study.

After the home was fully documented, inside and out, and before restoration could begin, post-Madison additions and fabrications needed to be removed. Workers removed portions of the interior trim, floors, framing, and fixtures—much of it to be recycled or reused—and then dismantled the twentieth-century exterior walls. With special care, all original Madison fabric was protected and set aside for analysis.

In the process of removing the later additions, the construction history of the mansion was confirmed and many more original Madison elements were discovered. Later owners, particularly William duPont, had conscientiously saved some Madison features, re-installing them or reusing them in new locations. By the end of the removal process, ten Madison-era windows, seventeen of the thirty-seven surviving doors, and two fireplace

TOP and MIDDLE: Architectural materials salvaged during deconstruction and original duPont fixtures are all part of Montpelier's collection. ABOVE: Floors were removed and saved, and this mantel was crated.

"Everywhere we had a question, it seems the house itself gave us the answers."

—*John Jeanes, director of restoration*

Workers carefully deconstruct later
additions to expose the Madison mansion.

mantels were discovered, having been recycled
within the mansion or moved to another location
on the property. Even wooden panels and boards
had been reused, and each gave more clues to
the appearance and character of the Madisons'
home. "Everywhere we had a question, it seems
the house itself gave us the answers," said John
Jeanes, director of restoration.

Restoring the Masonry

Montpelier's craftsmen first focused on restoring
the structural integrity of the home, starting with
its brick walls. Using hand tools to minimize
damage, masons carefully chiseled from the
original brick the stucco that was first applied
about 1855 and later reapplied in the twentieth
century. They then gently washed off the stucco
residue, exposing the hand-made, oversized
brick of the home's original exterior walls.
Every masonry wall was carefully evaluated and
stabilized—repairing the mortar, underpinning
foundations, and filling in openings created by
later doorways.

Wherever possible, the masons reused original

Madison bricks, but a number of new bricks were required. For this purpose, Old Carolina Brick Company carefully replicated the original bricks—hand-molding them to match the originals in size and firing them in temperature-controlled furnaces to replicate the colors of the older brick. Where an old brick was only partially damaged, masons carved a replacement piece from one of the new bricks and inserted it next to the surviving portion of the historic brick.

The lime for the original Madison-era mortar came from a limestone quarry on the plantation, apparently abandoned before the twentieth century. For the restoration, workers collected limestone from the same Everona limestone vein, located in the nearby town of Gordonsville. To re-create the mortar "recipe," masons and architectural conservators first analyzed the original mortar from all three building stages of the Madisons' home. Masons from Virginia Limeworks then burned the limestone in a kiln and added sand from the nearby Rapidan River floodplain—just as Madison had—to form a mortar identical to the original recipe.

TOP LEFT: Exterior restoration begins by stripping off stucco that had been applied over the outer brick walls. TOP RIGHT: The new mortar contains lime and sand from the same local sources as the original. ABOVE: Ray Cannetti cleans the mortar joints with compressed air.

OUR RESTORATION PHILOSOPHY

> Restoration was based on evidence—wherever possible from the house itself: the outline of a long-lost chair rail captured in the paint of the adjoining doorjamb; the stub of a newel post cut flush with the floor during a remodeling; the original shingles retrieved from the attic, where they had been dropped a century ago. Where post-Madison owners had reused an original feature, it was carefully returned to its original place or used to fashion an exact replica.

> Original material was preserved wherever possible. If elements—whether metal, wood, brick, or even window rope—were too deteriorated for use, they were cataloged and placed in storage.

> Where original fabric had to be replaced, matching materials (as close as possible to those employed in the period) were used. Throughout, high-quality antique wood was used, salvaged from a century-old mill in South Carolina.

> The highest quality craftsmanship was employed. Montpelier's restoration team represented the highest level of skill in the nation. Team members brought a deep knowledge of their professions and tools and a passion bordering on reverence for their work on Madison's beloved home.

PORCH WORK

To restore the front portico columns, masons first removed stucco from the underlying brick. They then rebuilt Madison-era brick bases, which had been partially cut away around 1855. After repairing any damaged bricks, the masons applied two coats of lime stucco to the columns.

Based on physical evidence, such as pockets (holes) in the masonry where the joists were originally installed, as well as existing Madison-era colonnade framing, carpenters reconstructed the front portico and back colonnade decks; for this and the reconstructed steps they, like Madison, used heart pine, which is highly resistant to rot.

Repairing Structural Timbers

At the same time, carpenters undertook repair of the home's structural timbers. Several major beams and joists were dangerously deteriorated. One massive beam in the oldest part of the home had been attacked by termites at both ends, eating deep into the timber. Carpenters carved out its rotten interior and glued in place a new beam to restore the strength of the original timber, while leaving its outward appearance

TOP LEFT Plaster removed from the pillars reveals the original brick. ABOVE LEFT: Master mason Wayne Mays pulls a running mold along the capital of one of the portico columns, creating a smooth, consistent surface by removing excess stucco. TOP RIGHT: A new brick is carefully matched to the originals. ABOVE RIGHT: Bricks are hand-shaped like slices of pie to create a test column.

unchanged. As work progressed, carpenters used hydraulic jacks and oak cribbing to return the floor framing to level, in some places raising it as much as 3.75 inches to its original position.

Reconstructing Wing Roofs

The restoration team was grateful that the duPonts' builder had frugally reused the older materials from the Madison home. For example, portions of the original rafters for Madison's north and south one-floor wing additions had been reused as floor joists in two offices added to the old bowling alley on the property.

Madison's serrated wing roofs were framed in a series of small ridges and valleys and then covered in decking. This type of roof, developed by Thomas Jefferson, was used to allow rainwater to run off while creating a usable flat terrace on top of the roof. Madison improved on Jefferson's design by covering his roof with iron sheeting, bought from inventory left over from the construction of the U.S. Capitol in Washington.

Montpelier's restoration crew faithfully replicated this design but covered the roof with stainless steel to ensure that leaks would not develop. The restoration team then installed wood

ABOVE: After the wing additions were demolished, the "serrated" roofs, based on Jefferson's design, were rebuilt on the east and west wings. This unusual design was used to create a deck on the roof, accessed from the second floor doorways. ABOVE RIGHT: A worker installs the Chinese railing on the north wing roof terrace.

decking on top of the serrated framing, just as Madison had, and painted it to match the original Spanish brown color, which was determined from a ridge of paint found on the brickwork. The final touch? Low, white Chinese railings, based on period images and the original building accounts.

Restoring the Wood-Shingle Roof

Restoration carpenters first peeled away the more modern copper roof to expose the roof framing. Once again, they found that time and

later changes had taken their toll. Roof leaks over the lifetime of the building had caused extensive rot in the heavy beams, and many lighter rafters and purlins had been cut off to accommodate later additions. Each beam was repaired, restoring its original length with similar wood that was carefully fitted in place with a complex but strong traditional joint. The old attic yielded a rich harvest of dozens of original wooden shingles, cut from heart pine and American chestnut. These shingles served as patterns for more than thirty thousand new shingles, all sawn, scalloped, and stained by hand. Old-growth cypress was selected for the roof shingles because of its extreme durability.

TOP: Peter Post carefully places one of the 30,000 shingles. ABOVE: The exact pattern, or "reveal" for the overlapping shingles is found in the weathered appearance of this original example.

SPLAY SQUINT SCARF JOINT SAVED THE DAY

A splay squint scarf joint similar to the one used to mend timber throughout the house. The joint is designed to be extremely strong under stress.

Repairing the Damaged Cornice

Much of the home's cornice, a major exterior architectural element, survived. Additional sections were discovered, reused as nailers in the attic. Where pieces of the molding had to be replaced, carpenters took profiles in order to exactly match the original. Where possible, they even straightened and reused the original nails, meticulously replacing them in their original locations.

Repairing Doors and Windows

Although many of the original Madison windows survived, most had suffered deterioration from more than two centuries of exposure to the elements. Carpenters carefully repaired each window to restore its original appearance and structural strength before re-installing it. Original locations were determined by carefully analyzing dimensions, matching the original paint with the paint in the rooms, and, in many cases, matching the nail holes found on the window frames to corresponding nail holes in the rough window openings.

The sidelights flanking the front door revealed a surprising innovation. Each was a movable window sash that disappeared into a pocket below, letting air into the vestibule. Painted shut for more than a century, each sash retained its Madison-era hemp rope. Investigators tracked down in the Netherlands

TOP RIGHT: Cornice after repair. ABOVE: The moveable window sashes flanking the front door.

comparable six-strand, six-millimeter hemp rope to match the original that was subsequently installed in all the windows.

But did the western breeze circulate and provide ventilation just in the front entryway? The question was promptly answered with the discovery that the corresponding interior sidelights, flanking the door into the Drawing Room, also proved to be movable, this time rolling not down, but left and right into side pockets fashioned inside the walls.

In just thirty months, Montpelier's team of skilled architects, architectural historians, and craftsmen had reached a major milestone: resurrecting the shape and exterior of President Madison's home from the covering of later additions and renovations. The completion of the exterior restoration was officially unveiled in April 2006.

INTERIOR RESTORATION

With the exterior restoration complete, the restoration team turned to the interior. There were sixty-one doorways in President Madison's house; remarkably, thirty-seven of those doors survived and were still on the property, although more than half were not in their original locations. Where were the doors hung during the Madison's tenure? The house itself revealed the answers through surviving nail holes, paint colors, and evidence found in the framing.

Restoring Interior Framing and Partitions

Some of the interior walls had been removed as the home had evolved. Clear evidence of the Madison-era partitions was revealed by mortises in floors and ceilings that once held wall studs in place. Historians carefully documented the missing studs, which preserved the location of not only the lost walls, but also the doors that

TOP: One of the main portico beams is put in place. MIDDLE: Sash cords survived from Madison's time. BOTTOM: Reinstalling an original window frame.

A Madison-era door opening, filled in by later owners, was revealed when plaster was removed.

pierced the walls. One interior wall, made of masonry, required a different approach: the location of a door was revealed only when the plaster was removed; the opening below it had been filled with newer brick.

Carpenters restored partitions in the 1764 and 1797 cellars, based on evidence from the joists that support the first floor. In the older 1764 space, carpenters sheathed the partitions with riven oak clapboards, as was common in the eighteenth century; in the 1797 Cellar, workers used beaded pine boards following the pattern of original boards that had been reused.

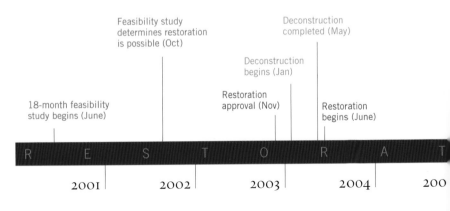

Feasibility study determines restoration is possible (Oct)

Deconstruction completed (May)

Deconstruction begins (Jan)

18-month feasibility study begins (June)

Restoration approval (Nov)

Restoration begins (June)

RESTORAT

2001   2002   2003   2004   200

OF MICE AND MEN

Who would have known what a treasure would be found in, of all places, a mouse's nest hidden behind a wall on the second floor? As the nest was carefully teased apart, its components were identified as a strip of upholstery fabric, a fragment of hand-painted wallpaper, a strip of newspaper, and a scrap of a hand-written letter. The date of the nest was confirmed when the handwriting of the letter was identified as James Madison's!

Behind another wall someone—or some rodent—had hidden the cone-shaped silver head of a candle snuffer. Madison-era decorative finishes also became evident in an unusual sassafras- or fig-leaf wall painting (ca. 1764) found beneath plaster on the second story of the original house.

Completion of the restoration
of the mansion interior

Constitution Day
September 17, 2008

mpletion of the restoration
he mansion exterior (April)

Décor research
and furnishing of
the mansion

O N   T I M E L I N E

2006   2007   2008   2009   2010

TOP: Modern conduit is hidden within a chimney. ABOVE: A massive underground bunker was constructed to remove from the house the modern amenities needed to provide security, fire control, and temperature and humidity control to protect museum objects.

Installing Modern Systems in an Old House

Modern mechanical systems do not hark back to the Madison period, but fire suppression, security monitors, and heating systems other than open fires are essential for a modern house-museum. To accommodate these realities without intruding on the spaces of the historic home, workers built a massive vault under the rear lawn. It was soon filled with electrical panels, air handlers, sophisticated temperature and humidity controls, fire control systems, and a "green" geothermal heating and cooling system. Engineers carefully extended these systems into the house to minimize their impact, placing them largely where the Madisons had placed their heating system—in the chimneys. These and existing brickwork chases were used to conceal much of the wiring and ductwork.

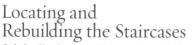

Locating and Rebuilding the Staircases

Originally the investigators feared that so little could be discovered about the two major staircases in the house—one from the original 1764 house and the other from the 1797 addition—that they would forever be "black holes." The stairs had been removed and replaced with new staircases during later renovations. But careful examination revealed just enough physical evidence to understand their placement, form, and style. The exact location, width, and rise and run were preserved in original framing and outlines. Then the restoration team found a reused piece of the original newel post for the later 1797 stair. Physical evidence for the earlier enclosed 1764 stair was also seen on the framing, and critical evidence for a first-floor landing was found on a reused door frame that originally led to the stairway. The overall design and style could be deduced from these clues.

LEFT: Mac Ward installs the stair spandrel (the paneling that runs between the skirt board and the floor). RIGHT: Farrar Woltz (owner of Acanthe Design) paints the faux grain on the railing of the north passage staircase.

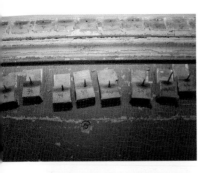

TOP LEFT: The disassembled dining room mantel. TOP RIGHT: Keith Forry cutting baseboard for the closets. MIDDLE: Mark Gooch installs glass in the portico's lunette window. ABOVE: Layers of paint form a "ghost" image of a chair rail.

Repairing Trim Work

Most of the Madison-era woodwork—flooring, mantels, paneling, baseboard, door frames, window surrounds, cornices, doors, and windows—survived. Some had been moved from their original locations. A typical example: a recycled baseboard was discovered holding laths supporting twentieth-century ceiling plaster. By analysis of dimensions, paint, and nail holes, and with the help of historic photos, architectural investigators determined each piece's original location and then turned it over to carpenters to be repaired and re-installed.

Chair rails were a different story. Originally a feature of virtually every room, they had been removed in the nineteenth century and

CANNETTI'S QUEST

In the Drawing Room, the 1880s installation of a marble fireplace mantel had partially demolished a Madison-era sandstone surround. But behind the mantel, the restoration team discovered the original material: St. Bee's red sandstone, which master mason Ray Cannetti tracked to a quarry—still in operation—near Cumbria, England.

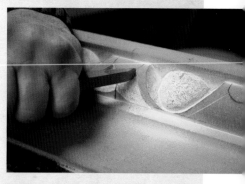

After importing replacement stone slabs, Cannetti hand-carved new elements to replace the severely damaged pieces, exactly matching the decorative egg and dart pattern.

The fireplace hearthstone provided another mystery. In the bottom of an 1880s sump hole in the cellars, archaeologists found a large stone slab. Upon examination, Cannetti recognized distinctive chisel marks on the bottom; they matched their cast counterparts still existing in the hearth's mortar bed. The slab was indeed the Madison-era hearthstone, which Cannetti carefully laid back in its honored place.

were long lost. Montpelier's investigators turned to the window and door frames to which these chair rails had butted. With careful, layer-by-layer removal of paint, the exact profile of almost every chair rail was fully recovered. The chair rails, which differed in design and height from room to room, were then re-created in heart pine and installed in their original locations.

TOP: Mason Wayne Mays nails lath to the ceiling of the second floor chamber. ABOVE: The plaster slumping through the back side of the lath. RIGHT: Following period recipes, George Dempsey adds horsehair to lime and sand to give tensile strength to the scratch coat plaster. FAR RIGHT: Tim Proffitt and Robby Kolb apply the ceiling finish coat of plaster in the upper passage.

Restoring the Plaster

The home had been almost completely replastered in the remodeling campaign of the early twentieth century. Because that plaster was a "modern" formulation that tended to hold moisture in the walls, it was completely removed. The original lath was mostly intact, and replastering began by ensuring that each strip of the old, hand-split lath was securely nailed in place.

Three coats of plaster were required to create the smooth finished walls and ceilings just as Madison's masons did. The first step was applying a thick "scratch" coat of plaster. Made of lime, heavy with sand, water, and incorporating horsehair, the scratch coat was pushed partly through the gaps between the lath,

HOW MUCH HORSEHAIR DOES IT TAKE TO RESTORE MR. MADISON'S HOUSE?

In restoring Montpelier to James Madison's home, some amazing numbers were tallied:

> **56 pounds** of horsehair mixed into the plaster
> **90 tons** of dry-mixed plaster mixed with water and horsehair
> **377,600 hours** of labor by skilled craftsmen and artisans
> **56,000 bricks**—each hand-molded and sand-struck—replaced damaged originals
> **30,000 old-growth cypress shingles** of varying widths—hand-scalloped and stained

> **23,739 square feet** of living space removed from the twentieth-century house
> **1,921 tons** of masonry rubble removed (1,480 tons of brick, 270 tons of plaster, and 171 tons of concrete)
> **2,300 pages** in the feasibility study
> **$24,000,000** spent restoring the home
> **206,400**—approximate number of visitors who witnessed the restoration in progress (January 2003—September 2008)

TOP: The plaster "scratch coat" on one of the upstairs bedrooms. ABOVE: Priming a window.

so it would slump through the spaces and lock onto the back side of the lath.

While still wet, the scratch coat was scored (thus its name) to provide a good binding surface for the second layer. The second coat, the "brown coat," formulated with lime, was used to create a flat, level surface on walls and ceilings. The third and final coat was made of refined lime and fine white sand, and was applied in a thin layer, creating the final smooth surface. This is further finished with applications of lime in water, consolidating the finish plaster, filling small voids, adding to the hardness and durability of the surface, and creating a white, lime-wash appearance.

In the 1797 addition and the 1809 Drawing Room, Madison's workers took a labor- and cost-saving shortcut by burnishing the second plaster coat rather than applying the third finish coat. Surviving evidence indicates that Madison then had these walls finished with wallpaper— in the Drawing Room—and a water-based brownish distemper paint in the 1797 addition.

Recovering Interior Finishes

Jack Fisher prepares a wall for the distemper paint.

The home also contained extensive evidence of the finishes of the walls and trim. Hidden behind an upstairs bed chamber in the oldest portion of the home was a fragment of plaster with a remarkable painted pattern. Other surviving fragments of the pattern indicate that it covered the entire surface below the chair rail of the room from 1764 until the Madisons' remodeling of 1810.

Extensive paint analysis determined that the baseboards in every room in the home were painted dark gray. Window and door frames also revealed their original colors and showed that an off-white "stone" color was used extensively. Evidence of water-based distemper paints was also found on some of the original plaster walls, especially in the 1797 addition. Restoration painters hand-ground pigments, mixed them with a binder and, using traditional oval-shaped and round animal-hair brushes called pencils, applied the paint to all the interior trim, re-creating the authentic "ropy" texture and gloss.

In the Madisons' Drawing Room, generations of painting and wallpapering did not quite remove evidence of the original finish:

in a small crevice above a window, a tiny, two-hundred-year-old remnant of red, flocked wallpaper was recovered. Other rooms also yielded evidence of wallpaper, and research on Madison-era wall coverings continues.

Repairing Floors

Although most of the Madison-era random-width flooring survived, it had been lost in two rooms in the oldest part of the home. In these rooms, carpenters installed new heart-pine flooring, determining the widths by surviving nail holes in the old joists. Elsewhere, where necessary, original floors were patched with carefully fitted plugs or "dutchmen," repairing damage caused by insects, wear and tear, and installation of heating and plumbing. Later stains and waxes were also removed, restoring the original finishes throughout. The unusual floors of the cellars carefully follow evidence recovered by archaeological teams: brick in the kitchens, wood in the 1797 cellars, and packed clay in the 1764 basement.

The restoration of the physical structure

TOP: **Keith Forry installs the floor.** MIDDLE: **Reproduction headless wrought nails are used in new floors.** ABOVE: **Undercutting a floor board with an adze.**

of Madison's home was deemed officially complete on Constitution Day, September 17, 2008. However, the restoration process never really ends. Historians and curators continue to research and analyze data that gives insight into room use, furnishings, and the Madisons' lifestyle. This is evident as we look at Montpelier as it is today.

ABOVE: Keith Forry installs patches in holes found in the floors. The irregular shapes of the heart pine "dutchmen" help them blend with the original surface. BELOW: Archaeologists Mark Trickett (left) and Brian Schneider (right) remove cement from Dolley Madison's cellar kitchen floor one five-foot square at a time, revealing the herringbone pattern of the original Madison brick.

CHAPTER 4
MONTPELIER TODAY

MODERN VISITORS TO MONTPELIER ENCOUNTER THE

same hospitality and beauty noted in the social commentary of

Dolley's friend Margaret Bayard Smith—but *without* the troublesome

travel conditions.

"Having lost ourselves in the mountain road
which leads thro' a wild wood track of ground,
and wandering for some time in Mr. Madison's
domain, which seemed interminable, we at last
reached his hospitable mansion."

—*Margaret Bayard Smith, 1828*

The Visitor Center for James Madison's Montpelier and William duPont Gallery.

PHOTOGRAPH BY PAUL KOZLOWSKI, COURTESY OF IMMCORE

EDUCATIONAL GALLERIES AND CENTERS

Madison's beautiful Montpelier estate welcomes you to a home and its grounds, a place of learning and discovery as history continues to unfold in a variety of venues, beginning with its Visitor Center.

The Visitor Center

With the opening of the Visitor Center for James Madison's Montpelier and William duPont Gallery on Madison's 256th birthday, March 16, 2007, Montpelier expanded its educational offerings, featuring presentations in four venues: the entrance lobby, the Alan and Louise Potter Theater, the Joe and Marge Grills Gallery, and the William duPont Gallery. The center also includes a café and a Museum Shop.

Entrance Lobby

The lobby of the Visitor Center introduces visitors to James Madison's Montpelier. A three-dimensional map portrays the terrain, the features of the property, and the walking path system, permitting visitors to quickly plan their visit within a time frame as short as one hour or as long as all day. Nearby, a timeline spans

the period from Madison's birth in 1751 to the end of his life in 1836, graphically showing his "place" in American and world history.

Alan and Louise Potter Theater

Visitors begin their tour in a comfortable sixty-seat theater, viewing a presentation on James Madison, the history of the plantation, and the restoration of the home. State-of-the-art technology can accommodate videos, digital presentations, and live demonstrations.

Joe and Marge Grills Gallery

The gallery features rare Madison personal items, valuable original Madison-era artifacts, and objects from the Montpelier plantation.

Small mementos, jewelry, china, archaeological finds, and other priceless possessions of James and Dolley Madison offer a glimpse into the Madisons' world.

TOP: The Joe and Marge Grills Gallery.
ABOVE: James Madison was a good friend of the famed portrait painter Charles Willson Peale, whose son Rembrandt painted a miniature of Madison, possibly from life. Watercolor on ivory.

William duPont Gallery

Adjoining the Visitor Center, The Montpelier Foundation preserves the history of Montpelier's other significant family—that of William and Annie duPont, and their children, Marion duPont Scott and William duPont, Jr. During the family's residency, they established Montpelier first as a renowned country estate and then as a thoroughbred racing stable. The Gallery shows visitors what life was like during the duPont era and displays objects from that period. The Gallery also continues Montpelier's celebrated tradition as the center of a vibrant and hospitable social life with a Grand Salon for events, concerts, presentations, and dinners. The Gallery's Grand Salon includes special pieces from formal rooms added to the mansion in the duPont era: marble fireplace surrounds, chandeliers, a bookcase, a chinoiserie mirror, seating furniture, and a rare, restored upright Steinway piano—a wedding present for Annie duPont from her husband, William.

In addition, the William duPont Gallery

TOP: The Grand Salon showcases two elegant fireplaces, a chandelier, and furniture belonging to the duPont family. ABOVE: The 1893 Steinway "Upright Grand" piano was custom-made for Annie duPont.

contains the Art Deco Room created by Marion duPont Scott in the 1930s, carefully reinstalled and featuring original chrome trim, mirrors, and a glass mantel. The room is filled with trophies and photos of her beloved horses, just as it was in her lifetime.

Education Center

Originally a barn built for young Marion and brother Willie duPont's ponies, today Montpelier's Education Center serves as an exhibit hall for visitors. It features two exhibits.

One, titled "Public Places—Private Spaces: A Reflection of the Madisons at Montpelier," exhibits the furnishings of James and Dolley Madison and of James' parents, Nelly and James, Sr. This exhibit delves into the process of investigating the history of furnishings. Some items on display were purchased at auctions held at Montpelier after the Madisons' residency; others, through family tradition, are believed to have been owned by the Madisons. Pieces on display include a ca. 1760 walnut corner cupboard, likely made in Fredericksburg; a ca. 1815 bedstead and bed steps; a ca. 1805 desk

TOP: Marion duPont Scott's Art Deco Room, meticulously removed from the mansion and reinstalled in the duPont Gallery.
ABOVE: ca. 1760 walnut corner cupboard, likely made in Fredericksburg, on display at the Education Center.

M. REMORENKO/DESIGN3

and bookcase, thought to have remained at Montpelier after Dolley sold the house in 1844; and a ca. 1765 walnut gate-leg table, believed to have been used by James as a study table at Montpelier. A vignette of the Madisons' Montpelier Dining Room encourages visitors to imagine that they have stepped back in time to November 17, 1824, when General Lafayette and his entourage came to Montpelier.

The second Education Center exhibit, "James Madison: Architect of the Constitution and the Bill of Rights," is a dynamic and visually stimulating presentation on Madison's role in the development, writing, and implementation of the founding documents of our democratic government.

ABOVE: The Education Center. BELOW: Exhibits detail Madison's role as Father of the Constitution.

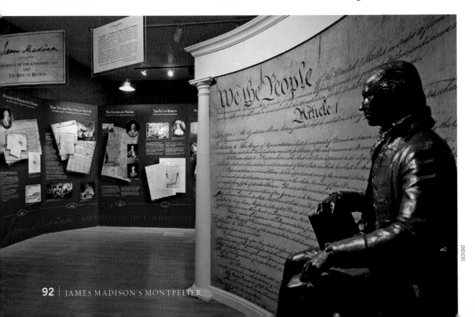

DESIGN3

THE MANSION

With the exterior and interior restoration complete, new questions came to the fore—not about the formulation of mortar or plaster—but about the character of the Madison rooms themselves. In the Madisons' retirement years— and as it stands restored today—the Montpelier mansion contained 7,768 square feet on the upper floors and 4,493 in the cellars. How did James and Dolley use the spaces in their home? How were their rooms finished and furnished? Where did distinguished guests stay? Answers to these questions draw us closer to sensing the people who lived within the plastered walls. But definitive answers aren't so easy to come by. The Madisons, like any home owner, used the rooms to serve their needs—which changed over time.

The re-creation of furnished rooms requires as much attention to detail as the restoration of a house's structure—which itself can supply clues to interior décor. What do nail holes in window casings reveal about window treatments? What do we learn from tiny scraps of wallpaper? How can these clues be used to better understand how

Montpelier curatorial consultants Lance Humphries and Susan Borchardt investigate the locations of paintings in the Drawing Room.

James and Dolley, their household slaves, and their many distinguished guests lived in the rooms of Montpelier? To develop a "room-use" and furnishings plan, Montpelier's curatorial staff and advisers supplement their extensive knowledge of the architecture, decorative arts, and social milieu of the early nineteenth century with the study of personal Madison artifacts and documents, written accounts of the family and of those who visited, visual records of period homes, and oral tradition.

As Montpelier curators work through this discovery process, the rooms themselves, as well as archaeological remains and written visitor accounts, give us insight into how the rooms were used and what they looked like—starting with the cellars.

The Cellars

Archaeological, as much as architectural, expertise unlocked the history of the vast Montpelier cellars. Perfectly preserved beneath

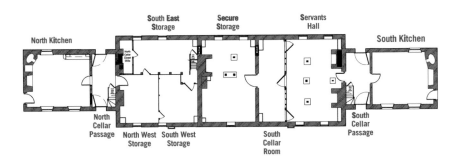

Floor plan of cellar.

a later concrete basement floor—carefully and laboriously removed with jackhammers and chisels—lay entombed remarkable evidence of room partitions, floor treatments, and storage pits dug in the floors for vegetables, personal items, and hearth ash.

The cellars of the similar wings on both sides of the house contained duplicate kitchens,

LEFT: The South Kitchen floor. The older bricks are the originals on which the simple running bond pattern was based. BELOW: The North Kitchen features semi-circular pocket windows, a hearth, and a set kettle (the arched opening to the right). Note the fancy pattern in the brick floor.

passageways, and stairs leading up to the first floor. In the South Wing, used by Mother Nelly Madison, the kitchen featured a wide hearth, an oven, and a brick floor laid in a simple running bond pattern. Its east and west walls featured semicircular windows that dropped into pockets deep in the brick walls, providing light and holding in warmth, when closed, and ventilation, when open.

In the North Wing, the kitchen was more modern. Its short hearth made room for a set kettle, which provided a constant source of hot water for the household, and a bread oven. The east wall held a wooden work station or dresser, as it was called at the time. The North Kitchen was floored with brick laid in a fancy herringbone pattern and had the same windows as the South Kitchen.

In the center portion of the house, the cellars

were divided: the portion under the original 1760s home, and the portion under the 1797 addition. The original southern portion was laid out with three rooms and had an earthen floor made from natural clays mixed with lime and tamped into a smooth, hard surface.

The windows in the main cellars were not covered with glass but with fixed bars that kept out animals and intruders but not cold weather.

The most southern room was partitioned into what was most likely a large Servants' Hall where slaves could carry out tasks, take their meals, and even rest while waiting to be called on during extended duty in the house. It included a fireplace that provided warmth and a place to cook food. Underground pits provided storage for vegetables and root crops as well as for ash to be used in making soap.

The other two rooms of the original 1760s cellars were probably used for storage. The Secure Storage was likely used for wine and other valuable supplies; it retains its original wooden door, complete with a time-worn key hole.

To the north of these three 1760s rooms lies the 1797 center cellars, the floors planked with wood. This area was divided into three large rooms, all of which were likely used for storage. In one, a barrel had been buried in the corner floor, probably to keep root vegetables cool.

The First Floor

Curators and restorers have begun unraveling the history of the first-floor rooms. Although no comprehensive household inventory exists, the Madisons' dinner or house guests—and there were many—wrote numerous descriptions of their visits to Montpelier. Several specifically described the first-floor public rooms, which, because of their social importance, feature more elaborate wood trim and more costly architectural features than private rooms.

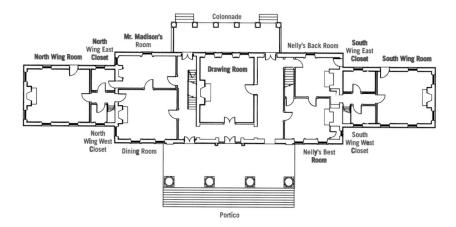

North Wing Room | North Wing East Closet | Mr. Madison's Room | Colonnade | Nelly's Back Room | South Wing East Closet | South Wing Room

Drawing Room

North Wing West Closet | Dining Room | Nelly's Best Room | South Wing West Closet

Portico

Drawing Room

Architecturally, the Drawing Room—elaborately trimmed with a cornice, a chair rail decorated with composition rosettes, a Venetian doorway, and sandstone mantel—is the center of the house. Here the Madisons welcomed their guests; here the family and company gathered before dinner. The women returned here after dinner, leaving the men to their brandy and cigars. One visitor found Madison quietly reading here in the morning. While Madison was president, a visitor wrote of playing chess in the Drawing Room.

In 1828, Margaret Bayard Smith, an astute commentator of her day, described the Drawing Room furnishings: "The mantelpiece, tables in each corner and in fact wherever one could be fixed, were filled with busts, and groups of figures in plaster, so that this apartment had . . . the appearance of a museum of the arts."

In 1832, John Latrobe mentioned "two immense mirrors"; "numerous paintings, some quite large, procured by Paine Todd, when he was in Europe"; "a piano . . . in one recess; an electrical machine occupies a corner"; and "the finest statue in bronze of Napoleon at Elba, with the figure of Icarus upon the pedestal, that I have ever seen."

ABOVE: Floor plan of the first floor. BELOW: Drawing Room details.

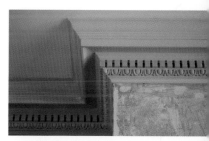

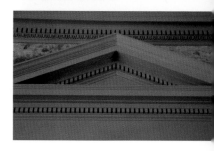

WHAT'S THAT ON THE WALL?

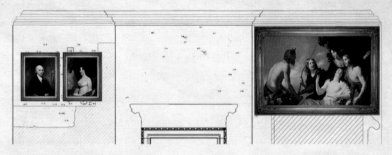

"We were shown into the drawing room, which might without great impropriety be called a little gallery of paintings."

—From the *Salem Gazette*, November 20, 1835

Fortunately, soon after James' death, an inventory was taken of fifty "Oil Paintings at Montpellier" and amended when Dolley Madison moved to Washington. Using this list in combination with visitors' accounts of their Montpelier memories, the known existence of six of the original paintings, and the nail-hole pattern in the original plaster of the Drawing Room, the curatorial team sleuthed out the probable hanging scheme of the Madisons' impressive painting collection in the Drawing Room.

Where are the six original works today? Five—Gilbert Stuart portraits of George Washington, Thomas Jefferson, and James and Dolley Madison, and a John Vanderlyn portrait of James Monroe—are in the collections of major institutions: the Colonial Williamsburg Foundation, the White House, and Clarkson University. Using the latest digital technology, these have been reproduced for Montpelier.

A seventeenth-century European depiction of a scene from Greek mythology, *Pan, Youths & Nymphs*, by Gerrit van Honthorst, was successfully traced from Dolley's estate to its 2004 sale at auction in Amsterdam. The Montpelier Foundation hopes to one day see this painting return to its place on the north wall of Montpelier's Drawing Room.

One striking painting still eludes researchers. Standing eleven feet tall—virtually floor to ceiling—and depicting the biblical scene *Jesus Appearing to His Disciples Peter & Cleophas* or *Supper at Emmaus,* by Belgian artist Charles Spruyt, it was sold in 1851 by John Payne Todd. Who knows where the investigation will lead?

South Passage

Almost an extension of the Drawing Room, the wide South Passage also displayed art, described by John Latrobe as "paintings of various merits and demerits." The cross ventilation, from doors in both the front and back, would have made the South Passage a pleasant space for sitting, reading, and conversing. Most of the paneling in the South Passage is original.

Nelly's Best Room

Madison's mother, Nelly, lived in the South Wing of the house until her death in 1829. Nelly's "Best Room," which featured wood

paneling, is likely where she received guests— what we today might call her living room. Nelly seems to have retained three south rooms as her own, with a dining room and bed chamber as well as the Best Room.

Nelly's Best Room.

After her death, Nelly's Best Room was converted into a sculpture gallery, described by

John Latrobe as containing "a collection of casts, chiefly busts, many of which are very good—as Joel Barlow, Paul Jones, Clay, Mr. Madison himself, and John Quincy Adams." This again shows the extent of the Madisons' interest in and collection of art.

The Madisons' Dining Room

On the other side of the Drawing Room, after passing through the narrow North Passage, guests would reach the Dining Room—home to

The Dining Room's mantel in its original location. Removed in the 1880s, the long-lost mantel was donated to Montpelier by Orange County residents Mr. and Mrs. Randolph Thompson.

many a grand feast—which, a visitor mentioned, could comfortably seat up to fifteen or twenty. Here sumptuous meals were served to all who visited the "Sage of Montpelier;" here the men lingered after dinner, discussing topics such as crops, politics, trade, and prose. Slaves had direct access, using the stairs outside the Dining Room to ferry food and wine from the Cellar.

Fortunately, an inventory of the contents of the Dining Room was created a few days after

HIDDEN IN THE MIDDEN:
THE PRESIDENT'S PLATES

As part of the project, archaeologists found and carefully excavated a midden, or trash pile. Located in a ravine about two hundred feet from the kitchen on the north side of the house, the midden was created as house slaves threw away scraps from the table, broken bottles and china, worn-out utensils, and other debris. Archaeologists discovered more than a dozen fragments of a dessert plate made by the Sèvres manufactory of

Paris for a member of the court of King Louis XVI and Marie Antoinette. The fragments match a surviving plate donated to Montpelier by a Madison family descendant, confirming family traditions that linked the service to the French royal court.

The trash heap also revealed fragments of another set of china, the Madisons' Nast porcelain dinner service, purchased in France in 1806 for the Madisons by Fulwar Skipwith, the American consul general. Apparently, after the White House was burned, President Madison used the 231-piece Nast service in Washington as his "state" china.

The midden has revealed many fragmentary treasures that will provide clues to refurnishing the house: molded teawares, English blue-and-white transfer-printed plates and serving pieces, stemware, table glass, and chamber pots. Remains from consumables, such as Champagne bottle fragments and wire stays, bones from prime cuts of meat, and oyster shells give clues to the Madisons' diet and affluence.

James' death. The purpose of the inventory is unclear, but it has proven extremely helpful as curators search to discover the room's artwork collection of thirty-six prints and its tables, sideboards, and many silver pieces.

Mr. Madison's Room

In James' final years, the room behind the Dining Room was converted into his study. It also served as a sitting room, where he rested during the day—as documented by guests who noted James' entrance to and exit from dinner. This is where he continued organizing his papers after he was confined to his bed, where he met with notable visitors later in his life; it is also the room in which he died, surrounded by the books and papers that meant so much to him in life.

Mr. Madison's Room.

"I was conducted to the apartment of Mr. Madison. He had, the preceding season, suffered so severely from rheumatism, that, during this winter, he confined himself to one room, rising after breakfast, before nine o'clock, and sitting in his easy-chair till ten at night . . .

The active old man, who declared himself

*crippled with rheumatism, had breakfasted,
risen, and was dressed before we sat down
to breakfast. He talked a good deal about the
American presidents and some living politicians
for two hours, when his letters and newspapers
were brought in."*

—Harriet Martineau, 1835

*"The last few years of his life, his fingers were so
affected by rheumatism that he dined at his small
table, in this room (having his dinner cut for him)
placed sufficiently near the door of the dining
room for him to converse with his guests."*

—Mary Cutts, Dolley's niece

Second Floor

The second floor of the home provided
bedrooms for family and guests. Curators are
scouring old letters, newspaper accounts, and
other documents to determine exactly what these
rooms looked like, and who slept where. The
stairs in the 1764 portion of the house ascend
to an open hall or passage, with a large storage
closet lined with shelves. Two rooms to the south
served as bedrooms, and one provides access
to the spacious Terrace, as it was termed by
visitors, over the South Wing. The large, central
bedroom gave honored guests outdoor access

Floor plan of the second floor.

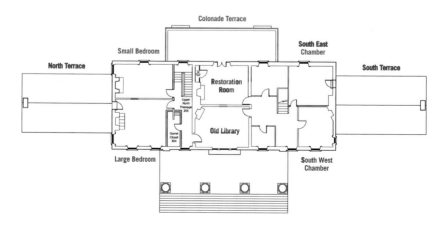

to the Colonnade Terrace. Because the central bedroom—now called the Restoration Room—holds such a concentration of architectural evidence, it has been only partly restored, preserving the clues and discoveries that guided the Montpelier restoration.

Madison's Library

Before he became president in 1809, James used the front, center upstairs room as his library; this "Old Library" may have also been the library in his father's house. It was in this

room where Madison researched past attempts at self-government prior to the Constitutional Convention. It was in this room, with its magnificent view of the western Blue Ridge Mountains, that James Madison read, thought, and devised a plan that would make the very first successful constitutional democracy, a republican form of government that would be thriving more than two hundred years later.

TOP: The Large Bedroom. ABOVE: A detail of the mantel in the Large Bedroom.

Northern Bedchambers

On the north end of the house, in the 1797 addition, are two rooms. The Small Bedroom has its own fireplace. The more prominent Large Bedroom, with a fireplace, ample light, and access to the North Terrace, features an original mantel embellished with a composition ornament that was molded in Washington, D.C. Its central decoration illustrates a Greek goddess of fortune and fertility (Fortuna) riding in a chariot with a putto (a young male child) and holding a cornucopia.

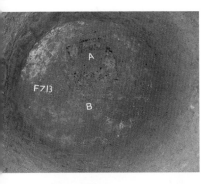

A

F7I3

B

THE ESTATE
The Grand Entrance

Today's visitors to Montpelier approach the mansion along the road that Madison built to create a dramatic distant view of his home.

From the foot of the hill in front of the home the carriage driveway was rerouted by later owners before the Civil War. In 2006–2007, Montpelier archaeologists unearthed evidence of the Madisons' front gate and fence by

TOP: Posts in the 19th-century were charred to slow decay, leaving remains that allowed archaeologists to determine the fence location. ABOVE: Illustration showing the location of the fence, disembarking area, and carriage road.

locating and carefully excavating its postholes, each with intact remains of the base of the original four-inch-square fence posts.

Inside the recently reconstructed fence, an area paved with Rapidan River gravel mirrors what archaeologists found inside the curved portion of the fence. Madison installed this to serve as a mud-free area for carriages to pull in and passengers to disembark. The main carriage road, in front of this stone pavement, extended as a dirt road from the Temple on the north to the original farmstead to the south beyond the current Visitor Center. Today a footpath follows the original

CARRIAGE RUTS
PRESERVED IN THE ROAD

Montpelier archaeologists never dreamed that they would uncover the Madison-era fence and road complex, perfectly preserved down to the last set of wagon ruts in the road! But landscaping changes about 1848 serendipitously provided a front-yard "time capsule." That was when new owners of Montpelier lowered the ground surface in front of the Portico to allow for a driveway directly to the house. The soil removed from this area was deposited on top of the old Madison front-yard road. The cover of soil perfectly preserved the remains of the road, the paved carriage siding, and even the last set of wagon ruts for archaeologists to uncover some 160 years later.

In most areas, the Madison-era landscape is no more than six inches from the surface and has minimal disturbance. Archaeologists also discovered the charred remains of the posts that demarcated the fence line evident in a 1817 watercolor. The bottoms of the posts were charred prior to installation to harden them from insect infestation. This charring left a perfectly preserved footprint of the fence and even allowed archaeologists to identify the wood species of the posts—black walnut and locust.

Madison road, from the Visitor Center to the carriage siding, where the front gate opens to a gravel path leading to the mansion's front Portico.

Mr. Madison's Temple

"On the right hand a short walk from the house was a beautiful temple, surmounted by a structure of Liberty; it was built over the icehouse which made it very cool; close to it was an immense mulberry tree, this building was intended, but never used, for his study."

—Mary Cutts, Dolley's niece

Mr. Madison's Temple.

While living in Washington, looking forward to summer recess if not retirement, James envisioned a classically inspired gazebo. For a preliminary sketch of what is known as Mr. Madison's Temple, James turned to William Thornton, architect of the Capitol. (The Temple is also similar to a "monopteron" temple drawn about 1804 by Thomas Jefferson, possibly intended for Monticello but never built.) To build the Temple, Madison had his workmen remove his father's ironworks, located north of the house close to where the Temple stands today, and extend the formal lawn of the mansion grounds. Construction was completed in 1811.

Its eight brick columns were covered with stucco and supported a wood-shingle roof. Flooring joists and clean-laid wooden flooring survived until the early twentieth century, when they were replaced by a concrete platform.

The graceful, contemplative structure is a fitting symbol for Madison, encompassing his love for the classics, his appreciation for architectural beauty, and his practical nature. For beneath the Temple, he had workers dig a twenty-three-feet-deep ice well that facilitated the summertime luxury of serving cool drinks and ice cream.

One ice pond still exists just down the hill from the Temple. In winter, workers cut ice slabs, hauled them by horse and wagon, lowered them into the ice well, and packed them with straw to keep them for summer retrieval. At the base of the Temple, facing the pond, a small brick arch marks the top of the original entrance to the ice house (now filled in with brick). Today the entrance is no longer accessible.

Aside from the main house, the Temple is the only intact Madison-era building on the property. Local friends and tourists enjoy summer concerts and family activities staged in front of the Temple, and many a bride has promised eternal love in front of its majestic columns.

TOP: The excavated foundation of the shared chimney for a duplex slave residence in the South Yard. ABOVE: Detail of an artist's rendering of domestic slave quarters.

Domestic Slave Quarters

Just south of the mansion, enslaved domestics lived and worked in a service complex called the South Yard, which today is marked with a sign as a visitor stop. A map created as part of an insurance policy purchased by Dolley in 1837 revealed the existence of this group of structures. Archaeologists found eighteenth-century remains of the early detached kitchen (a brick foundation and hearth), evidence of one slave quarter, and a filled-in well. They are now searching for traces of the other slave residences and smokehouses shown on the insurance map.

During the James, Sr., era, the South Yard was visually separated from the formal yard by buildings and a wall. Living quarters were very crudely built—most likely log structures with clay floors and stick and mud chimneys. Household refuse was discarded down the back slope.

James and Dolley reconfigured the South Yard, replacing the older cabins with framed quarters with raised wooden floors, glass windows, and brick chimneys. A large double hearth in one excavation indicates the residence was a duplex, housing two slave families, as documented on the insurance map. The areas between the residences

WHAT MAKES A CHAMPION TREE?

In the official measurement system, a tree is awarded points based on its circumference in inches plus height in feet plus one-quarter of the average crown spread in feet.

Montpelier's prize English Oak stands 65 feet tall with a circumference of 192 inches and an average crown spread of 76 feet—scoring 276 points. (The former champion, in Loudoun County, scored 219.)

The Osmanthus stands 33 feet tall with a circumference of 33 inches and an average crown spread of 23 feet—scoring 72 points. (The former champion, in Norfolk, scored 61.)

The Spanish Fir stands 50 feet tall with a circumference of 130 inches, and an average crown spread of 47 feet: scoring 192 points. (The former champion, in Richmond, scored 156.)

were likely work yards, and the slaves used two parallel paths paved with brick and stone to reach the mansion and its cellar kitchens.

Champion Trees

James Madison was Montpelier's most famous resident, but a few current residents continue to make headlines. Three Montpelier trees are state champions in their species category, as determined by the Virginia Big Tree Program—a cooperative group comprising the Virginia Forestry Association, the Virginia Department of Forestry, and the Virginia Polytechnic Institute's College of Natural Resources.

All three award-winning trees stand on the southwest side of the mansion. The gnarly English Oak (Common Oak) and the stately Spanish Fir grace the lawn. The twisted

Montpelier's champion English Oak.

Osmanthus (Holly Leaf) is rooted just inside the woods along the trail to the visitor parking lot.

Are there more champion trees at Montpelier? Possibly so. More trees still need to be surveyed.

Annie duPont Formal Garden

Following William duPont's purchase of Montpelier in 1901, Annie duPont transformed two acres of the original four-acre Madison garden into a contemporary formal garden, restoring terraces; planting flowers, shrubs, and trees; and adding brick walls, statuary, and ornamental iron gates. Marion duPont Scott made additional changes. She commissioned noted landscape architect Charles Gillette to design brick walks and perennial herb beds; she also introduced a number of unique plants such as the golden arborvitae. The Garden Club of Virginia undertook the restoration of the garden in 1992, returning it to its early-twentieth-century glory as a formal flower

TOP: The rambling Osmanthus (Holly Leaf) forms a secret hiding place beside the trail to the Visitor Center. ABOVE: The towering Spanish Fir in winter.

garden, as created by Annie duPont. The flower beds incorporate many varieties of bearded and Japanese iris, daylilies, and peonies, along with other plants common to the period.

James Madison Landmark Forest

"Nearly all the way I rode under a vault of green . . . the rich vegetation of a thousand kinds of gigantic trees, a virgin soil, studded with young shoots, and renewing through them, in the crumbling corpses of the majestic pines and haughty oaks."
—Montpelier visitor, Baron de Montlezun, 1816

A two-hundred-acre wood behind the house has been designated a National Natural Landmark by the U.S. Department of the Interior, as the best and largest old-growth forest surviving in the southeastern Piedmont. It is similar to the original forests that once blanketed this region. It exists in part because Madison appreciated the value of forests, in 1818 noting,

TOP: The Annie duPont Formal Garden is graced by a pair of lion sculptures.

"Of all the errors in our rural economy none is perhaps so much to be regretted . . . as the injudicious and excessive destruction of timber . . . It seems never to have occured that the fund was not inexhaustible."

The James Madison Landmark Forest has an array of species distinctive to the Piedmont and is accessible by two miles of trails that have been carefully placed to avoid damage. The forest is protected by an easement held by the Nature

Conservancy and is managed as a wilderness area. Nonnative plants are removed; trees are cut only to keep the interpretive trail open. Otherwise nature takes its course in this unique forest.

The rich, red soil and moist climate of the Southwest Mountains of Virginia's Piedmont provide an ideal environment for deciduous hardwood trees. The tulip tree is the tallest and dominant tree within the forest, reaching heights of 125 feet. Its lifespan is 250 to 300 years. American chestnut trees once thrived in the forest until blight destroyed them in the early twentieth century. Decayed remains of the chestnuts can still be found, forming hollow logs on the forest floor. Red oaks grow almost as tall as tulip trees and can live two hundred years. White, black, and chestnut oaks also thrive here. These trees, as well as pignut and mockernut hickories, white ash, and beech create the highest canopy of leaves, or overstory, of the forest.

Trees and shrubs that grow well in shade—including flowering dogwood, redbud, spicebush, and pawpaw—form the understory, or lower canopy, of leaves. Wildflowers such as black cohosh, Solomon's plume, cutleaf toothwort, and

WHAT IS AN OLD-GROWTH FOREST?

Three important characteristics make an old-growth forest:
> It consists largely of native plant species—those that have evolved in this region.
> It has grown without significant human intervention.
> Many of its trees have reached their maximum lifespan.

Artist's rendering of the Farm Complex. From left, field slaves' quarters, tobacco barn, overseer's house, more quarters and a Madison-era road can be seen.

putty root, grow on the forest floor.

In Madison's day the well-traveled Mountain Mill Road, along the southeast edge of the forest, linked Montpelier to a gristmill, which ground the plantation's wheat and corn. What remains of the Mountain Mill Road serves as the foundational route of four interpretive pedestrian trails through the forest.

Farm Complex

Adjacent to the Visitor Center, along the trace of the Madison Mill Road that extended to the original Mount Pleasant farmhouse, archaeologists discovered the heart of Madison's agricultural complex: quarters for field slaves, barns, and other work areas. When Dolley Madison sold Montpelier in 1844, the area was abandoned and the structures decayed. Amazingly, this entire Farm Complex field was never subsequently plowed, and it will provide archaeologists with rich evidence of the plantation's agricultural base.

The crude homes of the field slaves stood in marked contrast to the improved homes of the domestic slaves. Field-slave quarters were likely made of logs, with dirt floors, simple plank

shutters, and chimneys made of sticks and mud. The slaves built the homes themselves, receiving only nails and door hardware from the Madisons. Preliminary excavations already indicate that field slaves had fewer dishes and clothing than house slaves, perhaps due to less time for producing and selling marketable items.

Houses for Montpelier field slave families would have looked much like this 1880s log home near Petersburg, Virginia, photographed by Frances Benjamin Johnston.

In the midst of the field-slave quarters, archaeologists also located the site of one of the Madisons' tobacco barns, strategically set on a ridge, in the path of available breezes necessary to dry the large tobacco leaves. An 1871 visitor's account cited the then-abandoned tobacco barn as the only extant building in the area, indicating that it had been well built, likely by James, Sr., to withstand inclement weather and protect the plantation's valuable cash crops.

Beeping metal detectors revealing nails and hand-forged tools? These clues led to the discovery of what are probably the workshops for Montpelier's carpenters, coopers, and wheelwrights. These structures were concentrated at the wooded edge of the mansion grounds (the wooded area to the rear of today's

Visitor Center). The view of this complex from the mansion was described by an 1832 visitor as,

"Peeping through the foliage near the house, you catch a glimpse, at some distance of the barns and farming arrangements of the Estate."
—John Latrobe, Montpelier visitor in 1832

Mount Pleasant Discovered

In a pasture adjacent to the Madison family cemetery lies the remains of the earliest settlement of Montpelier—built by Madison's grandfather, Ambrose—called Mount Pleasant. The Mount Pleasant site has yielded abundant clues of the compound: a root cellar (filled with

TOP: The excavated stone-lined kitchen cellar of the Mount Pleasant home.
ABOVE: Artist's rendering of the Madison' original home.

burnt structural debris) of a modest dwelling for the enslaved workers who cleared the land beginning in the 1720s.

Excavations also revealed a nearby stone-lined cellar containing the burned remains of the Madisons' original home. Lower deposits contained the fallen walls of the structure. But why were there virtually no trim nails or

hardware? The clay floor, "clean" except for a pile of charred peaches with their stems still intact, in what appears to be a wooden crate, suggested that the house had been stripped of any usable materials before it was intentionally burned, soon after being vacated in the 1760s. The only vestige of the home's elite status was the fragment of a decorative andiron recovered from layers of burnt wall plaster. Upper layers of the cellar contained dense ash deposits sprinkled with artifacts, including animal bone, eggshells, charred seeds, and shattered ceramics. It seems that a field-slave family that continued to reside in the old kitchen-turned-quarter used the cellar of the burned main house to dispose of refuse and hearth ash.

After the Madison family moved to Montpelier, one of the only structures remaining at the Mount Pleasant site was the detached kitchen. Lower levels of fill in the stone-lined cellar of the kitchen included six wine bottles, most bearing James Madison, Sr.'s, hand-blown glass seal, indicating the family's refined tastes and the use of the cellar for wine storage. Upper levels of fill indicated that the building was occupied by slaves following the Madisons' move to Montpelier and later destroyed by an accidental fire, which consumed the slave family's household contents; burned remains include thimbles, glass bottles, and ceramic plates, bowls, and cups.

Archaeologists and historical architects have diligently worked to discover the character of Ambrose Madison's house. It likely faced southeast toward the main road and was small, about twenty-six by twenty-four feet.

TOP: Reconstructed wine bottles were recovered from the kitchen cellar at Mount Pleasant, most bearing James Madison, Sr.'s seal. ABOVE: Archaeologist Melissa Rich assembles ceramics recovered from the burned remains of the kitchen/slave house.

TOP: A light snow reveals the depressions of unmarked gravesites in the Slave Cemetery. ABOVE: Artist's rendering of a slave funeral.

The Slave Cemetery

Nestled among trees, a few hundred yards from the Mount Pleasant site, archaeologists found forty grave depressions. None of the graves is marked with an inscribed stone, though some quartz or other fieldstones serve as head and foot markers. Such a large number of simple burials—though far from the total number of slaves that lived and died on the Madison property—points to this half-acre site being the main slave cemetery at Montpelier. The visible depressions that can still be seen in the cemetery mark the locations of the latest burials, graves in which the fill dirt would have "settled" after slavery was abolished and the community was no longer intact to maintain the burial grounds of its members.

Gilmore Cabin: A Freedman's Farm

Opened to the public in May 2005, after a two-year restoration, the Gilmore Cabin stands as the only preserved and interpreted freedman's home in the United States. Throughout much of the year, weekend guides give visitors an

opportunity to understand the transition from slavery to freedom for African Americans across the south after the Civil War.

George Gilmore was born a slave at Montpelier around 1810. Emancipated as a result of the Civil War, he and his wife, Polly, secured land from Dr. James A. Madison, a grandson of James' brother. Archaeology has revealed that before 1870, Gilmore built a cabin from remains of a deserted Confederate camp. (The structure was later used as a workshop or kitchen.) By 1872, the Gilmores had the resources to build a new one-and-a-half-story cabin in their "front yard," again "recycling" the stones from the initial chimney. As restored, the Gilmore farm includes the 1872 house, a vegetable garden, and hog pen.

The 1880 census lists Gilmore as a farmer, rather than a laborer, indicating he farmed his own land. Hundreds of glass beads, buttons, and safety pins discovered under the flooring and in the firebox affirm the family's oral history—that Polly Gilmore worked as a seamstress.

In 1901, George Gilmore completed the purchase of the sixteen-acre farm from Dr.

TOP: The Gilmore Cabin. MIDDLE: The cabin before restoration. ABOVE: The interior gives a glimpse into the daily life of the Gilmore family in the 1870s.

JJ ⋁ 26

GILMORE FARM

George Gilmore was born into slavery at Montpelier about 1810. Like millions of African Americans throughout the South, Gilmore made the transition to freedom after the Civil War. Many emancipated slaves worked on the same plantations where they once labored. Gilmore, his wife Polly and five children lived in this cabin built by family members in 1873 and farmed the surrounding fields. In 1901 George Gilmore obtained the deed for 16 acres from Dr. James A. Madison. After Gilmore's death in 1905 the property remained in the family until 1920. Archaeological and architectural investigations have resulted in the restoration of this rare example of a surviving freed family's cabin.

Madison. For freedmen, land ownership helped secure not only sustenance, but also a community, independence, and stability. George died in 1905; both he and his wife are buried on their farm. Their descendants occupied the cabin into the 1930s, although they had earlier sold most of the land to William duPont. The remaining three acres, still owned by Gilmore family members, were donated to The Montpelier Foundation in 2006. A historical highway marker was erected on the site in 2006.

Civil War Trail

In the woods behind the Gilmore Cabin, Montpelier archaeologists—aided by local relic hunters—located and excavated portions of a regimental Confederate Civil War encampment. The encampment housed General Samuel McGowan's South Carolina Brigade during the winter of 1863–1864, when it was part of an extended defensive line along the nearby Rapidan River. The camp was abandoned on May 4, 1864,

TOP: Rebecca Gilmore Coleman, great-granddaughter of George and Polly, speaks at the dedication of the Gilmore Farm historical marker in 2006. ABOVE: Items discovered during the cabin's restoration.

when McGowan's 1,500 men set off for the Battle of the Wilderness, where the Brigade suffered higher than 30 percent casualties.

Covering a five-acre area, the camp was located near water but with good drainage. Huts were laid out in streets, with a company officer positioned at the top of each street. Eleven rows of ten huts ran from the top of the ridge, down-slope to the northwest.

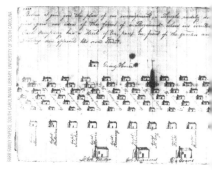

Archaeologists excavated four hut sites at the regimental camp featured on the interpretive trail. Excavations revealed the soldiers made their fires directly on the clay floor of the huts, leaving a tell-tale area of scorched clay for the hearth location. Between the huts, pits provided clay for daubing the chimneys and logs and later served the combined purpose of water sumps and trash pits. The scarcity of material goods recovered from these trash pits—nothing more than small nails and burnt clay that washed down the clay-lined chimneys during rainstorms and then was swept from hearths—attests to harsh living conditions. Most of the remnant stoneware—jugs and crocks—was manufactured in South Carolina, suggesting troops obtained few items from local merchants.

TOP: An 1862 sketch of a South Carolina camp shows a layout similar to that of the Montpelier encampment. MIDDLE: Hiking Montpelier's Civil War Trail. ABOVE: Archaeological excavation of two hut sites.

CONSTITUTIONAL BREAKTHROUGHS

After the Civil War, the Thirteenth (1865), Fourteenth (1868), and Fifteenth (1870) Amendments to the Constitution abolished slavery, gave citizenship to anyone born in the United States, and extended voting rights to freed slaves. James Madison's constitutional framework—allowing for amendments—paved the way for this expansion of civil rights.

The National Park Service has recognized the camps at Montpelier as the only known encampments of their size and condition on protected land. Given the extent and preservation of these camps, which housed as many as 2,500 men during the winter of 1863–1864, new finds will continue to uncover additional information regarding Montpelier's Civil War era.

Montpelier's self-guided Civil War walking trail connects the McGowan camp to the Gilmore Farm. By following the three-quarter-mile trail past the Confederate site and to the Gilmore Cabin, visitors can explore the period that carried our country through the war to emancipation and citizenship for enslaved African Americans.

The Madison Family Cemetery

"The remains of Mr. Madison lie in the adjacent family cemetery with those of his father and his mother by his right side, and room on his left for those who may follow him. Many relatives are interred within the same enclosure, which is covered with box and ornamental trees, and the whole surrounded by a neat brick wall."
—Letters of a Convalescent, 1839

If the mansion is the heart of the Montpelier property—the focal point of the celebration and interpretation of James Madison's life—the Madison Family Cemetery might be called the

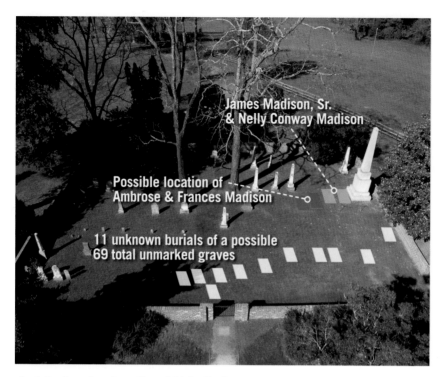

James Madison, Sr. & Nelly Conway Madison

Possible location of Ambrose & Frances Madison

11 unknown burials of a possible 69 total unmarked graves

plantation's soul, as its walls enfold the final resting place of James and Dolley as well as many members of the extended Madison family. Between 1732 and 1938, as many as one hundred people were laid to rest here. Only one gravestone commemorates an individual from outside the Madison family, that being Frank Carson, who lived at Montpelier during the Civil War.

The cemetery's proximity to the original Mount Pleasant home reflects its age. The oldest burial is presumably that of James' grandfather, Ambrose (d. 1732). Other early unmarked graves are those of Ambrose's wife, Frances (d. 1761); James' parents, James, Sr. (d. 1801), and Nelly (d. 1829); five of James' siblings who died as infants or children; and James' adult brothers Ambrose (d. 1793) and William (d. 1843).

Inscribed gravestones name thirty-one buried individuals, including James and Dolley and one of his siblings: Sarah Madison Macon (d. 1843).

ABOVE: The gate to the Madison Family Cemetery. RIGHT: The grave markers of Dolley (left) and James Madison (right).

The gravestones commemorate family and descendants of three of the president's siblings: Ambrose, William, and Sarah. William's lineage is buried in the southern portion of the cemetery; Sarah's family is clustered around her marker, north of William's section; Ambrose's descendants (along with those intermarried with William's) are buried farther north, near the president's grave. The earliest gravestone is dated 1811, but its style suggests it was set as late as the 1840s. The latest stone marks the 1938 burial of Susan Daniel Madison, the great-great-great-granddaughter of Ambrose.

The two most prominent grave markers, against the northern wall, commemorate President James and Dolley Madison. June 29, 1836, the day after James' death, pall bearers carried his body here to its resting place, to the left (north) of his parents' graves. The grave was unmarked until 1857; with the setting of the existing obelisk made of James River granite, the enclosed grounds no longer served as a private family site. The cemetery became inextricably tied to the nation that looked to the shrine as a visible connection to the almost mythical history of James Madison as the last of the Founding Fathers.

In 1999, the Virginia Chapter of the Daughters of the American Revolution launched a successful effort to raise funds for the restoration of the family cemetery, strengthening their long history of preserving the site since the 1930s. The circa 1810 brick wall around the cemetery was restored, and every grave stone and monument was stabilized and cleaned. The massive monument over Madison's grave had tilted; it was carefully underpinned to provide a stable foundation. Every year on Madison's birthday, March 16, a contingent of U.S. Marines lays a wreath from the U.S. president on Madison's grave.

Dolley (d. 1849) was initially buried at Washington's Congressional Cemetery. Her final wish—to be brought to Montpelier—was not realized until 1858. An 1839 newspaper account mentions there being room for another grave, inside the brick wall, on the president's left. But the large monument added in 1857 had cut into that space. Dolley was buried as close as possible to her husband—behind him. Her gravestone was carved by John W. Davies, who had previously constructed the presidential obelisk.

A CONTINUING JOURNEY

As man and woman, James Madison (1751–1836) and Dolley (1768–1849) have closed parentheses around their life dates. Even so, their legacy lives on, not in direct descendants, but in their writings, in interpretations of their influence, in their stately home looking out over nature's stunning handiwork.

Our understanding of James Madison's legacy and its critical place in our country's foundational political structure beckons us to continue our journey—to discover more about the great man who fathered a great ground-breaking document: the Constitution of the United States of America.

FURTHER READING

The following titles are presented for those who wish to further explore the lives and contributions of James and Dolley Madison and the history of the founding of our nation.

JAMES MADISON

Lance Banning, *The Sacred Fire of Liberty: James Madison and the Founding of the Federal Republic*

David Holmes, *The Religion of the Founding Fathers*

John P. Kaminski, *James Madison: Champion of Liberty and Justice*

Ralph Ketcham, *James Madison, a Biography*

Ralph Ketcham, ed., *Selected Writings of James Madison*

Richard Labunski, *James Madison and the Struggle for the Bill of Rights*

Drew R. McCoy, *The Last of the Fathers: James Madison and the Republican Legacy*

Jack Rakove, ed., *Madison's Writings*

Jack Rakove, *James Madison and the Creation of the American Republic*

Robert Rutland, *James Madison, the Founding Father*

James Morton Smith, ed., *The Republic of Letters: The Correspondence Between Thomas Jefferson and James Madison, 1776–1826*

J. C. A. Stagg, Series Editor, *The Papers of James Madison*

Garrett Ward, *The Political Philosophy of James Madison*

DOLLEY MADISON

Holly Shulman and David Mattern, *Dolley Madison: Her Life, Letters, and Legacy*

David B. Mattern, Dolley Madison, and Holly C. Shulman, *The Selected Letters of Dolley Payne Madison*

Catherine Allgor, *A Perfect Union: Dolley Madison and the Creation of the American Nation*

THE CONSTITUTION

Akhil Reed Amar, *America's Constitution, A Biography*

Akhil Reed Amar, *The Bill of Rights: Creation and Reconstruction*

Carol Berkin, *A Brilliant Solution: Inventing the American Constitution*

Catherine Drinker Bowen, *The Miracle at Philadelphia*

Forrest McDonald, *Novus Ordo Seclorum: The Intellectual Origins of the Constitution*

Gordon S. Wood, *The Making of the Constitution*

MONTPELIER

Jayne Blair, *Tragedy at Montpelier*

Bryan Clark Green, Ann L. Miller with Conover Hunt, *Building a President's House*

T.O. Madden and Ann L. Miller, *We Were Always Free: The Maddens of Culpeper County, Virginia, A 200-year Family History*

Ann L. Miller, *The Short Life and Strange Death of Ambrose Madison*

The Founding

Carol Berkin, *Women in Colonial America*

Susan Dunn, *Dominion of Memories: Jefferson, Madison and the Decline of Virginia*

Joseph J. Ellis, *American Creation: Triumphs and Tragedies at the Founding of the Republic*

Joseph J. Ellis, *Founding Brothers: The Revolutionary Generation*

John Hope Franklin and Alfred A. Moss, Jr., *From Slavery to Freedom: A History of African Americans*

Robin D.G. Kelley, Ira Berlin, Marc Favreau, and Steven F. Miller, *Remembering Slavery and Emancipation*

Stuart Leibiger, *Founding Friendship: George Washington, James Madison, and the Creation of the American Republic*

John P. Leffler, Richard Kaminski, *Federalists and Antifederalists: The Debate Over the Ratification of the Constitution*

Jon Meacham, *American Gospel: God, the Founding Fathers, and the Making of a Nation*

Gordon S. Wood, *Revolutionary Characters: What Made the Founders Different*

Gordon S. Wood, *The Creation of the American Republic, 1716-1787*

Children and Youths

Jean Fitz and Tomie de Paola, *Shh! We're Writing the Constitution*

Jean Fritz, *The Great Little Madison* (for adolescents)

Anne Kamma and Pamela Johnson, *If You Lived When There Was Slavery in America*

Hunter H. McGuire, Jr., *A Little Boy Who Taught Big Bullies to Behave*

We the People

of the ...
... insure domestic Tranquility, provide for the common defence, ...
... and our Posterity, do ordain and establish this Constitution for ...

Article

Section. 1. All legislative Powers herein granted shall be vested ...
of Representatives.

Section. 2. The House of Representatives shall be composed of ...
in each State shall have Qualifications requisite for Electors of the most ...
... Person shall be a Representative who shall not have attained ...
... and who shall not, when elected, be an Inhabitant of that State in which ...

Representatives and direct Taxes shall be apportioned among the ...
Numbers, which shall be determined by adding to the whole Number of ...
not taxed, three fifths of all other Persons. The actual Enumeration sh...
and within every subsequent Term of ten Years, in such Manner as the...
thirty thousand, but each State shall have at Least one Representative...
entitled to chuse three, Massachusetts eight, Rhode Island and Prov...
eight, Delaware one, Maryland six, Virginia ten, North Carolina fi...

When vacancies happen in the Representation from any State...
The House of Representatives shall chuse their Speaker and oth...

Section. 3. The Senate of the United States shall be composed of tw...
Senator shall have one Vote.

Immediately after they shall be assembled in Consequence of...
of the Senators of the first Class shall be vacated at the Expiration of the...
Class at the Expiration of the sixth Year, so that one third may be chosen...
...of the Legislature of any State, the Executive thereof may make temp...
such Vacancies.

No Person shall be a Senator who shall not have attained to th...
...when elected, be an Inhabitant of that State for which he shall be ch...

The Vice President of the United States shall be President of the...
The Senate shall chuse their other Officers, and also a President...
President of the United States.

The Senate shall have the sole Power to try all Impeachmen...
of the United States, the Chief Justice shall preside: And no Person shall...
Judgment in Cases of Impeachment shall not extend further th...
Trust or Profit under the United States: but the Party convicted shall ...
according to Law.